INSIGHT COMPACT GUIDES

Northumbria

D1611138

ALS No.

This item should be returned on or before the last date stamped above. If not in demand it may be renewed for a further period by personal application, by telephone, or in writing. The author, title, above number and date due back should be quoted.   LS/3

Star Attractions

An instant reference to some of Northumbria's top attractions to help you set your priorities.

Cragside p18

Warkworth Castle p24

Embleton Bay p26

Bamburgh p27

Kielder Water p35

Housesteads Fort p40

Durham Cathedral p45

Beamish Museum p51

Raby Castle p55

Teesdale p57

Killhope Lead Mining Centre p59

NORTHUMBRIA

Northumbria – Land of Far Horizons

Opposite: Rothbury locals

In Northumberland alone, both heaven and earth are seen; we walk all day on long ridges, high enough to give far views of moor and valley, and the sense of solitude far below... It is a land of far horizons, where the piled or drifted shapes of gathered vapour are for ever moving along the furthest ridge of hills, like the procession of long primeval ages that is written in tribal mounds and Roman camps and Border towers, on the breast of Northumberland.

The Cheviots' rolling slopes

The words of the great British historian George Macaulay Trevelyan, born and raised at Wallington House, near Cambo, encapsulate the moody, meditative spell which Northumbria still casts over its visitors.

History is everywhere in these bleak, northern hills – the last flourish of the Pennines before they cross the Border into Scotland. The great rolling slopes of the northern Cheviots are littered with so many settlements, enclosures, forts, cairns and field systems that you can be left in no doubt that these now-empty hills once supported a large and thriving farming population. Even today, the numerous sheepfolds that dot the landscape are known by the Norse word *stell*. Despite the more recent addition of alien conifer plantations which cloak so many valley sides, inland Northumbria and the North Pennines remain an uncompromising landscape of bleak uplands which have been adopted and adapted by Man over many centuries, yet which still manage to retain that sense of ultimately untamed wildness which has always been a feature of this Border Land.

Embleton Bay   **5**

Northumbria was a grim posting for Roman soldiers stationed at a high Cheviot camp or along Hadrian's Wall. But it appealed to the early Christian missionaries, who always based themselves in the remotest places. When they set out to convert the Northumbrians, it was no accident that they chose lonely Lindisfarne, today just one of many attractions along the Northumbrian coast. This beautiful coastline boasts not only some of the best and most unspoilt beaches in Britain, but also many of the area's castles, all fine examples of medieval military architecture. They range from the commanding presences of Alnwick, Bamburgh, Warkworth and Lindisfarne, presiding over their attendant settlements, to the evocative ruins of Dunstanburgh rising above glorious Embleton Bay.

Location and landscape

For the purposes of this book, Northumbria is the counties of Northumberland and Durham from the Scottish Border south to the great cathedral city of Durham and the line of the A688 and A66 which threads through the Stainmore Gap. It excludes the Tyneside cities of Newcastle and Sunderland, but takes in the whole of the Northumberland National Park, the Northumberland coast, the North Pennines Area of Outstanding Natural Beauty, and most of the Border Forest Park including Kielder Forest.

The landscape of the area is dominated by the great north-south barrier of the Pennines and Cheviots, which lie to the west, and the beautiful Northumberland coast-line to the east. The Pennines, along with the sandstone escarpment of the Simonside Hills, were formed during the Carboniferous Period about 300 million years ago, as layers of sandstone and limestone were laid down under the sea in warm, semi-tropical conditions. Later earth movements uplifted this 'sandwich cake' of gritstone and limestone layers into the familiar Pennine Dome, which has been eroded to its present elevated plateau by aeons of wind, frost and rain, most recently during the last Ice Age 10,000 years ago. Gaseous intrusions of minerals into the cracks and cavities of the limestone of Weardale deposited the lead ore which made the North Pennines a centre of industrial activity during the 19th century.

Violent volcanic interludes were responsible for some of the most outstanding physical landforms. Examples of these are the great granite bosses of the Cheviots, the much-eroded stumps of former volcanoes, and the intrusive quartz dolerite cliffs of the Whin Sill, along which the central stretch of Hadrian's Wall marches, and on which the castles of Holy Island, Dunstanburgh and Bamburgh were built. The impressive waterfalls of Teesdale, notably High Force and Cauldron Snout, also crash over outcrops of the same Great Whin Sill. The final sculpting of the landscape was accomplished by Ice Age glaciers which carved out the broad valleys of the Tees, Wear and the North and South Tyne.

The North Tyne above Kielder

Deforestation has been occurring as long as farming, but reforestation is a much more recent phenomenon, particularly on the scale seen in the massive conifer plantations of the Border Forest around Kielder, at the head of the North Tyne. Here the largest man-made forest in Europe has Kielder Water, its largest reservoir, at the heart of a totally unnatural landscape, which is nevertheless popular with many visitors. Both developments were made to serve short-term needs – the timber of the forest to alleviate war-time shortages and the reservoir to supply water to the industries of Teeside after an over-optimistic forecast of a boom. Upper Teesdale also suffered from a forecasted need for water, when the botanically-rich limestone pastures of the upper dale were flooded by the Cow Green Reservoir in 1970.

Cow Green Reservoir

Economy

Farming, particularly of sheep and cattle, is still the most important industry in Northumbria, as evidenced by the many sheepfolds of the Cheviots and the weekly markets held in the towns of Rothbury, Hexham and Middleton-in-Teesdale. Quarrying of stone for aggregate has taken over from lead mining as the major extractive industry in Upper Teesdale, although it is not on the same scale as in the Yorkshire Dales.

Today, tourism is becoming increasingly important to the local economy, and initiatives such as the North Pennines Tourism Partnership are attempting to bring more visitors to this largely unheralded and unspoilt outpost of the Pennines, dubbed by the authorities as 'England's Last Wilderness'. Further north, the designation of Hadrian's Wall as a World Heritage Site in 1987 threw the international spotlight on this splendid relic of the last northern outpost of Rome. The proposal to create a Hadrian's Wall long-distance path along its length will undoubtedly bring more pressure on the area, as did the creation of the Pennine Way, which opened up areas of the North Pennines and Cheviots to many more walkers in 1965. But is it still possible to find peace in the 'Empty Quarter' of the Northumbrian uplands.

Last outpost of Rome

When the Emperor Hadrian came to Britain during a tour of his western provinces in AD122, he decided that it was time to draw a permanent line to mark the northern boundary of the empire. He ordered the building of a wall, 80 Roman miles long, between the Solway Firth and the Tyne, in the words of his biographer, 'to separate the Romans and the barbarians'. The result was one of the most impressive examples of Roman military archiecture in Europe – and the finest and best-preserved Roman monument

Beaming at Beamish

Hadrian's Wall at Cuddy's Crags

The emperor Hadrian

The bath house at Chesters Roman Fort

Roman elegance at Chesters

in Britain. Hadrian's Wall still runs for 73 modern miles (117km) across the neck of northern England, and the best-preserved sections which mark the southern boundary of the Northumberland National Park were internationally recognised as a World Heritage Site in 1987.

The man who was charged by Hadrian with the building of this 'final frontier' was his new British governor, Aulus Platorius Nepos. The massive construction work was completed in only six years and, contrary to popular belief, not by slave labour but almost entirely by soldiers from the three Roman legions based in Britain. The Wall was a masterpiece of civil engineering, utilising the natural geological defences of the Whin Sill escarpment in its spectacular central section, and necessitating the building of bridges over two major rivers, the North Tyne and the Irthing. It has been estimated that, at today's prices, the cost of the Wall's construction would exceed £100 million – and would probably take just as long.

Only the eastern and central sections of the Wall (about 45 miles/72km) were built from locally-quarried sandstone. Because of the speed of the operation and the lack of suitable stone in the western section between the River Irthing and the Solway, the Wall here was built of timber and turf blocks, with stone-built milecastles and turrets at intervals. When completed, the Wall was about 16ft (5m) high and 9½ft (3m) wide. The embankments and flat-bottomed ditch of the *vallum* were a kind of de-militarised zone for people approaching from the south, while to the north a deep, defensive ditch was dug.

It is estimated that about 10,000 auxilliary soldiers from all over the Empire manned the Wall. Of the 12 forts along its line, the best-preserved and best known is Housesteads or *Vercovicium* on the most spectacular central section. The forts were garrisoned by at least 500 soldiers, and the smaller milecastles and turrets by about 24 men each. The Wall was finally abandoned around AD410 when the troops were withdrawn to defend the threatened Roman homeland. Outside the forts, such as at Housesteads and Vindolanda just south of the Wall, thriving civilian settlements or *vici* sprang up, trading with the Roman forces in a friendly fashion far removed from the constant warfare often described.

The Steel Bonnets

For something like 300 years between the late 13th and early 17th centuries, the Border reivers or Steel Bonnets, named after their metal helmets or burgonets, waged constant, unrelenting warfare across the Border hills.

According to their most eloquent chronicler, George MacDonald Fraser, it was a time when 'no man who lived between the Scottish Southern Uplands and the Pennines could walk abroad unarmed in safety; no householder in all the Marches could sleep secure; no beast or cattle could be left unguarded'.

It was a time when the tribal leaders of the Border counties – the Armstrongs, the Bells, the Charltons, Elliots, Johnstones, Grahams, Robsons and Nixons – made their own laws and in their own phrase, 'shook loose the Border'. And it was a time when, if the lady of the house presented her husband with a dinner plate on which was a pair of spurs, the laird knew that the larder was empty and it was time to ride out on another cattle-raiding foray.

Reivers on the rampage

The Border reiver was a unique figure in English history. He was a kind of rustic gangster who might come from any social class. He could be a peer of the realm or equally a farm labourer, but the one interest they shared was that they were all professional cattle-rustlers. In addition, according to Fraser, the reiver was 'a fighting man who, on the evidence, handled his weapons with superb skill; a guerilla soldier of great resource to whom the arts of theft, raid, tracking and ambush were second nature'.

To combat the constant raiding by the reivers, special defensive structures were built, and many still remain to be seen in the Northumbrian landscape. A typical village in reiver country is clustered defensively around the village green, where cattle could be herded when the Steel Bonnets called. The classic example is Elsdon in Redesdale, where there is also one of the finest examples of the so-called vicar's pele – a fortified house which doubled as a refuge in times of trouble.

Elsdon: solid masonry for siege protection

More evidence of those troubled times can be found elsewhere in the Northumbrian countryside in the remains, often ruinous, of the so-called bastle houses – semi-fortified farmhouses where the upper floor accommodated the hapless farmer and his family, and the lower his stock. Good examples can be found in North Tynedale in the valley of the Tarset Burn a few miles northwest of Bellingham, where the Black Middens Bastle has been restored by English Heritage. The Woodhouses Bastle in Coquetdale is another bastle in a good state of repair.

Black Middens Bastle

The reivers not only left their mark on the landscape, they left it in the language too. The name 'reiver' or reaver is now obsolete but meant a robber or raider, and significantly lingers on in the language as the root of the word 'bereave'. And it was the reivers who gave us the word 'blackmail', which was originally meant 'black rent', a kind of protection money paid by a tenant or farmer to a prominent reiver so that he would be left alone.

The violence was not finally stamped out until the 1603 Act of Union united the crowns of England and Scotland, and the subsequent appointment of Border Commissioners made the stealing of cattle punishable by death.

Historical Highlights

10,000–4,000BC Mesolithic people set up seasonal camps along the North Sea coast, and hunting parties visit the Simonsides and other Fell Sandstone hills. The first Neolithic farmers move into the valleys and lowlands such as Coquetdale and the lower Breamish Valley.

4,000–1,000BC The first metal workers of the Bronze Age move into the uplands of the Cheviots, leaving behind their burial mounds and cairns, for example those on Dour Hill, Knock Hill and Thirl Moor, and they carve the enigmatic cup-and-ring stones at Lordenshaws.

1,000BC–AD70 The Votadini tribe of the Iron Age construct about 150 hillforts throughout Northumberland, for example at Yeavering Bell, Brough Law and Lordenshaws. They are probably used as much as summer shielings as defensive positions.

AD79–81 The Romans under Julius Agricola enter Northumberland and construct the first wooden forts along the line of the Stanegate road at Corbridge (*Corstopitum*) and Chesterholm (*Vindolanda*) and northwards along Dere Street at High Rochester (*Bremenium*) and Chew Green (*Ad Fines*) high on the Cheviot ridge.

100 The Emperor Trajan withdraws the Roman troops from the Forth-Clyde frontier to Stanegate, between the Tyne and Solway.

122 Hadrian visits Britain and orders the construction of a wall under the supervision of Aulus Platorius Nepos, 'to separate the Romans from the Barbarians'.

130 The Wall, running 73 miles (117km) from the Solway to the Tyne, is completed, and stands for 300 years as the northern boundary of the Roman Empire until political instability at home results in the Wall garrisons being reduced and finally abandoned around 410.

547 The Saxon chieftain Ida wins control of the fortress of Din Guoaroy or Bamburgh, and sets it up as the capital of his new northern kingdom of Bernicia, which is united with neighbouring Deira 40 years later under King Aethelfrith.

616 Aethelfrith's successor Edwin marries Ethburge, a Christian princess of Kent, and 11 years later is baptised by the Roman missionary Paulinus in York, and sets up his palace of Ad Gefrin in the Glen Valley beneath Yeavering Bell.

635 King Oswald defeats Welsh and Mercian invaders at the Battle of Heavenfield, near Hexham. St Cuthbert is born in the Tweed Valley and St Aidan is sent from Iona to be Bishop of Lindisfarne.

664 Cuthbert becomes the Prior of Lindisfarne following the Synod of Whitby, and 20 years later is invited by King Ecgfrith to become Bishop of Lindisfarne. He dies in 687 on Inner Farne.

675 The first Hexham Abbey is founded by Wilfrid; after being sacked by Danish raiders a year later, it is refounded as an Augustinian abbey in 1113.

c700 Lindisfarne Gospels written. In the later years of the 8th century, the monastery is regularly attacked and sacked by Danish Vikings causing the monks to abandon it in 875.

995 Monks end their wandering with Cuthbert's body at the 'White Church' at Durham, on the site of the present cathedral.

1022 The Venerable Bede's remains are brought to Durham from Jarrow.

1066 The Norman Conquest. Three years later, William the Conqueror puts down a rebellion inspired by Danes and Northumbrians. In 1072 the first Durham Castle is built by William.

1080 The Harrying of the North is organised from Durham by Bishop Odo of Bayeaux. Every field and dwelling between York and Durham is laid waste, and every town destroyed except Bamburgh. About this time the motte and bailey castle is built at Elsdon.

1093 Construction of Durham Cathedral started by William of St Calais.

1165 Premonstratensian abbey founded at Blanchland.

1166 The Augustinian Lanercost Priory is founded by Robert de Vaux.

1309 Alnwick Castle becomes the principal seat of the Percy family.

1314 Dunstanburgh Castle built.

1377 Henry, fourth Lord Percy of Alnwick, is made the 1st Earl of Northumberland.

1388 The Battle of Otterburn, in which Scots under James Earl of Douglas defeat Harry 'Hotspur' Percy, son of the 1st Earl of Northumberland. Fourteen years later, another Scots force is defeated at the Battle of Humbleton Hill.

1513 Scots defeated by an English force led by the Earl of Surrey at the Battle of Flodden Field.

1566 On tour in the Borders, Mary Queen of Scots, still married to Lord Darnley, visits her next husband-to-be, Lord Bothwell, as he is holed up in Hermitage Castle after sustaining a wound in a border skirmish.

1585 Border disputes come to a head after the murder of Lord Francis Russell at a Wardens' Meeting at Windy Gyle in the Cheviots, but are largely dispelled by the union of the crowns of England and Scotland in 1603.

1725–26 Causey Arch, near Stanley, constructed – the oldest surviving railway bridge in the world.

1752–57 General Wade raids Hadrian's Wall to construct his parallel Military Road to counter the threat of a Jacobean invasion.

1815 The London Lead Company sets up its headquarters in Middleton-in-Teesdale, and five years later, constructs the model village of Nenthead in the South Tyne Valley for its employees.

1838 Grace Darling and her father, the keeper of the Longstone lighthouse, rescue nine passengers from the grounded steamer 'Forfarshire' off the Northumbrian coast.

1905 Construction of Catcleugh Reservoir completed in Upper Redesdale to supply water for industrial Tyneside.

1911 The War Office buys 19,000 acres (7,700 hectares) of land at Otterburn in Redesdale for military training.

1940–70 Planting of Kielder Forest, incorporating the Kielder, Falstone, Wark and Redesdale Forests into what becomes the largest man-made forest in Europe.

1956 Northumberland National Park is designated, covering 398 square miles (1,030 sq. km). Two years later, the Northumberland Coast Area of Outstanding Natural Beauty, covering 52 square miles (135 sq. km) between Amble-by-the-Sea and Berwick, including Holy Island and the Farne Islands, is designated.

1965 Tom Stephenson's Pennine Way is opened, a 270-mile walking route from Edale in the Peak District up the Pennines across the Scottish Border to Kirk Yetholm, passing through the Wark Forest and along the Cheviots.

1967 Cow Green Reservoir is proposed in Upper Teesdale, attracting widespread criticism from conservationists and nature lovers. Three years later, the dam is completed and the reservoir fills, drowning important Arctic-Alpine plant communities in Upper Teesdale.

1978 North Pennines Area of Outstanding Natural Beauty, covering 765 square miles (1,983 sq. km) between the Yorkshire Dales and the Stainmore Gap, is designated.

1982 Kielder Reservoir – the largest man-made lake in Europe – is completed, to serve the forecasted industrial needs of Teeside.

1987 Durham Cathedral and Castle and Hadrian's Wall Military Zone are both designated as World Heritage Sites by UNESCO for the importance of their cultural and archaeological landscapes.

1990 Hadrian's Wall National Long Distance Walking Trail is proposed, following the line of the Wall from the Solway to the Tyne.

1997 Northumberland National Park Authority is reconstituted. Public enquiry opens into Ministry of Defence plans for a major redevelopment of its Otterburn ranges.

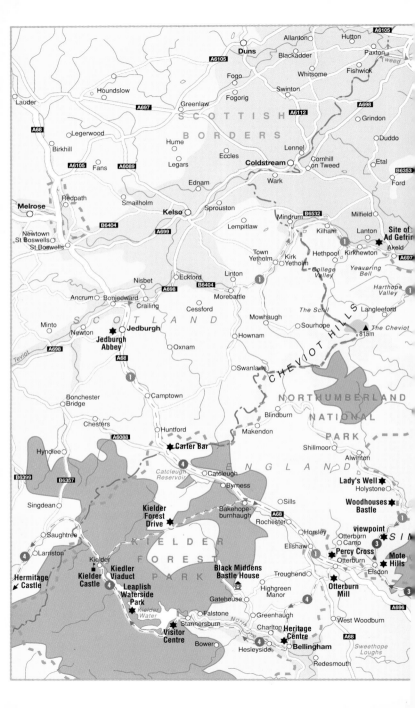

Preceding pages:
on the beach at Bamburgh

Wild White Cattle p22

15

Alnmouth p24

Hermitage Castle p35

The Cheviots from the Alnwick–Rothbury road

At home in the hills

Route 1

Around the Cheviots

Alnwick – Rothbury – Elsdon – Otterburn – Carter Bar – Jedburgh – Kirk Yetholm – Wooler – Chillingham – Alnwick (100 miles/161km) *See map, pages 14–15*

Born of a violent, volcanic past some 380 million years ago, the Cheviots are a quite distinct and separate entity from the Durham Dales and the North Pennines. Their rounded, usually grass-covered summits, which reach to well over 2,000ft (610m), stand aloof and proud beyond the valley of the Coquet in a massive 350 square mile (900 sq. km) boss of solidified lavas and granites. Local people know them as 'the White Land' in recognition of the pale, almost frosted colour of the rough grass which covers them. But their summits, particularly the reigning summit of The Cheviot itself (2,676ft/815m), are anything but white – they are covered with a sticky black, cloying blanket of peat, notorious to exhausted Pennine Wayfarers on the final leg of their 270-mile (435km) marathon from Edale in Derbyshire.

This 100-mile (161km) route encircles the Cheviots, and provides regular views of their summits. There are various opportunities along the route to stop, don the walking boots, and explore some of their valleys, because that is really the only way to explore their secrets.

The route starts in the pleasant little market town of **Alnwick** (pronounced 'Annick'), an important commercial centre for the area since the granting of its market charter in 1291. Mercifully by-passed by the A1 trunk road, Alnwick retains the air of a medieval town, with narrow,

winding ways and a cobbled ★ **Market Place**, complete
with stepped Market Cross. The **Old Cross Inn** in Nar-
rowgate is known locally as 'Dirty Bottles', in reference
to a row of blackened bottles which have stood untouched
in its bow window for nearly 200 years. Parts of Alnwick's
ancient town walls, begun in 1434, still exist, notably the
Hotspur Gate (closed to the public), named after the most
famous member of the local Percy family, Shakespeare's
Harry Hotspur. At the end of June each year, Alnwick
relives its ancient past in its Fair Week, with costumed
street processions, entertainments and an ox roast.

Dirty Bottles

   Alnwick's strategic importance on the crossing of the
River Aln was first recognised by the Normans who built
the first ★★★ **Alnwick Castle** (Easter to end of September, daily 11am–5pm, house from noon, last admission
4.30pm) in the 11th century. The famous Border family of
the Percys, Earls of Northumberland, lived here from 1309,
but the earldom became extinct when the last Percy died
without a male heir in 1670. The appearance of the present building, with its magnificent barbican, towers and
battlements, dates mainly from the 19th-century trans-
formation carried out by the 4th Duke of Northumberland.
The refurbishment earned the castle the title 'the Wind-
sor of the North' in Victorian times, and the interior is filled
with wonderful works of art, from paintings by Titian, Van
Dyke and Caneletto to beautiful furniture and an exquis-
ite collection of Meissen porcelain. The ★ **Regimental
Museum of the Royal Northumberland Fusiliers** is
housed in the Abbot's Tower, while the Postern Tower contains a collection of early British and Roman relicts collected from the surrounding area. The grounds of the castle
park were landscaped by Launcelot 'Capability' Brown,
a Northumbrian from Kirkharle, near Wallington. The Pastures below the castle are the scene of the annual Shrove
Tuesday Football Match, which uses the Lion and Den-
wick bridges over the Aln as goals.

Alnwick Castle

From Alnwick, take the B6341 southwest towards Rothbury, passing after about 5 miles (8km) a lay-by on the
right which, on a clear day, offers stunning ★★ **views** of
the Cheviots away to the west. At the bottom of the hill,
in a beautiful, secluded valley, lies ★ **Edlingham Castle**
(English Heritage, open all year, any reasonable time), a
complex ruin with a 13th-century hall and house, 14th-
century courtyard and 15th-century domestic tower.

Edlingham Castle

   Crossing the A697, the route enters the ancient bounds
of Rothbury Forest, a royal hunting forest from the 11th
to the 13th centuries, later passing into the hands of the
Dukes of Northumberland. It then descends sharply
through the modern, monocultural conifers of Rothbury
Forest into Rothbury. Just before the town, on the left, is

Cragside House and gardens

★★★ **Cragside House** (National Trust; 28 March to end of October daily except Mondays, house: 1–5.30pm; grounds: 10.30am–7pm; 1 November to 14 December, Tuesday, Saturday and Sunday 10.30am–4pm). This fantasic, mock-Tudor, mock-medieval building is a Victorian creation by the 1st Lord Armstrong, and stands in 900 acres (350 hectares) of landscaped gardens above the Debdon Burn, famous for their early-summer show of rhodedendrons and azaleas. Take time to follow the so-called 'Power Trail' through the gardens, a 1½-mile (2.5km) circular walk which includes the restored ram and power houses which provided the power to make Cragside the first house in the world to be lit by hydro-electricity, and the Armstrong Energy Centre.

Rothbury itself, the 'capital' of Coquetdale, is a pretty, bustling little stone-built market town constructed on a series of natural terraces above the north bank of the River Coquet. Clustered around its central green, it is a convenient holiday centre for the exploration of the Cheviots and nearby Simonside Hills. There is a ★ **Northumberland National Park Visitor Centre** in Church House in the Main Street (daily mid-March to end of September). The ★★ **Parish Church of All Saints** has a 13th-century chancel and transepts, but suffered from an over-enthusiastic restoration in 1850. Note the 17th-century font, which stands on the vigorously-carved remains of the 9th-century Rothbury Cross, the head of which is in the Museum of Antiquities, Newcastle-upon-Tyne.

Rothbury

Rothbury offers many opportunities for good walks, including the two-mile walk to the prehistoric landscape of Lordenshaws (*see Route 3, page 31*), and then on to the ridge of the Simonside Hills (*see also Route 3*).

Follow the valley of the Coquet westwards from Rothbury on the B6341 passing through ★ **Thropton**. At the western end of this pleasant village of neat, stone-built houses is a 15th-century pele tower, now converted to a house. The 'Three Wheat Heads' public house is a reminder of the fertile nature of the soils of mid-Coquetdale, although little corn is grown there today.

Thropton: the Three Wheat Heads

After passing through **Warton**, **Flotterton**, **Caistron** and **Hepple** with the heights of the Simonside Hills away to the left, a minor road leads right towards the delightful village of **Holystone**. On the way, there is roadside parking for the short walk to ★ **Woodhouses Bastle**, one of the finest examples of a medieval bastle or defensible farmouse in Northumbria. Holystone itself is famous for its ★★ **Lady's** or **St Ninian's Well** (National Trust). The village takes its name from the former 12th-century priory of Augustinian canonesses, who were dedicated to the worship of the Virgin Mary, and the church is still dedicated to St Mary. Lady's Well, which may get its name from the canonesses, is in a copse of trees a short walk north of the village, and consists of a tranquil rectangular pool of clear water fed by a never-failing sparkling spring. A simple Celtic cross stands reflected in the pool in this sacred and atmospheric spot. On Easter Day, 627AD, it was the scene, according to legend, of a mass baptism of over 3,000 pagan Northumbrians by St Paulinus, the Roman missionary from Kent who also baptised King Edwin the same year. A statue of the saint stands at one side of the pool, while on the eastern side a rough stone marks the place where he knelt to carry out his conversions. It is also associated with St Ninian, a 5th-century apostle, but it may have been built by Romans, as it lies on the line of their road to Redesdale.

Lady's Well at Holystone

Back on the B6341, continue westwards to enjoy the splendid views from the **Billsmoor Viewpoint Car Park** before descending into the perfect little Northumbrian township of ★★ **Elsdon**.

Elsdon has all the classic features of a Borders settlement. Its stone-built, mainly 18th- and 19th-century cottages cluster protectively round its village green, where cattle were impounded for safety when the reivers called (*see pages 8–9*). As you enter the village on the left can be seen the earthworks of the ★ **Mote Hills**, a classic Norman motte-and-bailey castle built by the de Umfravilles in the early 12th century and abandoned in favour of Harbottle Castle in 1160. In the centre of the large, triangular village green stands the sturdy little ★ **Parish Church of St Cuthbert**, dating from the 12th and 14th centuries. Legend has it that, because it was the nearest consecrated ground, many of the English dead from the nearby Battle of Otterburn in 1388 were buried beneath the north wall.

19

Elsdon parish church

Parking at Billsmoor Viewpoint

Elsdon's Pele Tower

Over 1,000 skulls were discovered here in the 19th century. On the green near the church is Elsdon's famous ★★ **Pele Tower** (private), a classic and much-photographed example of a so-called vicar's pele or defensive house, part-vicarage and part-fortress, designed to repel Scottish raiders.

Three miles (5km) to the east, the B6341 joins the A696 to enter Redesdale at the historic village of **Otterburn**. Otterburn's place in history is secured by the dramatic events of 5 August 1388, when, in the fields to the west of the village, the Scottish forces led by James, Earl of Douglas, defeated those led by Harry 'Hotspur' Percy, eldest son of the Earl of Northumberland. The Battle of Otterburn, one of the most infamous of the Border battles, is commemorated by ★ **The Percy Cross**, in a copse of trees close to the A696 north-west of the village. **Otterburn Tower** (private), a much-restored fortified house to the north of the village, was probably in the ownership of the prominent Hall family at the time of the battle, and may have been subject to a seige by the Scottish forces before the arrival of the English. ★ **Otterburn Mill** (Monday to Saturday 9am–5.30pm, Sunday 11am–5pm) is an 18th-century mill which now produces tweed clothing and rugs, with an exhibition of textile machinery once powered by a water turbine.

The route now follows the valley of the River Rede, joining the A68 near Elishaw for about 15 miles (24km) past the former Roman settlement of *Bremenium,* present-day **Rochester**, which after nearly 2,000 years is still the headquarters for the extensive military presence in the area in the form of the army's Redesdale Camp.

Shortly after entering the blanket afforestation of the Redesdale Forest, the road passes through the tiny settlement of **Byrness** where the **Pennine Way** crosses in one of its most boring sections on its way north to the Border. Just beyond Bryness is the 1½-mile (2.5km) long ★ **Catcleugh Reservoir**, built in 1905 by the Newcastle and Gateshead Water Company to supply Tyneside. Navvies lived in separate prefabricated villages named after the two towns on either side of the Rede as the reservoir was built, and one of their wooden huts has been preserved on site.

Catcleugh Reservoir and tourists at Carter Bar

The A68 now ascends onto open moorland and up to the Scottish Border at **Carter Bar**, at 1,370ft (418m) the highest point on the route, often crowded with visitors enjoying the fine views of the Cheviot Hills and the lowlands of the Jed Valley in Scotland to the north. Continue to follow the A68 as it descends into the valley towards the busy and historic township of **Jedburgh**, which is reached after 13 miles (20km).

Ruined ★★ **Jedburgh Abbey** (Historic Scotland, open daily all year) was founded in the early 12th century and is famous for its fine rose window, known as St Catherine's Wheel, in its west front. Both Bonnie Prince Charlie and Mary Queen of Scots stayed in Jedburgh, in houses which have both been preserved as museums.

From Jedburgh descend into the valley of the Teviot, and turn right onto the A698 at **Bonjedward**, through **Crailing** and **Eckford**, to turn right again eastwards onto the B6401 following the valley of the Kale Water. With the slopes of the Cheviots rising away to the right, you pass through the village of **Morebattle** to **Town Yetholm** and its smaller neighbour ★ **Kirk Yetholm**. Here, the Border Hotel is forever remembered as the northern terminus of the **Pennine Way**, but the village has an interesting history of its own. Clustered around its pretty green, it was once a famous meeting place and camping ground for Romanies, and is where they chose to bury their last queen, Esther Faa Blyth, in 1835.

Continue north back across the border, turning right at **Mindrum** onto the B6351 through **Kirknewton**. The road runs close to the northern edge of the Cheviot Hills, soon passing the prominent dome of **Yeavering Bell** (1,182ft/360m) crowned by its Iron Age hillfort. On the opposite side of the road stands the rather ugly memorial overlooking the site of King Edwin's Saxon palace of *Ad Gefrin*, where he was baptized by Paulinus in AD627.

Joining the A697 at **Akeld**, the route now enters **Wooler**, a workaday farming and market town. Wooler gives easy access via **Yearle**, **Middleton** and the delightfully-named hamlet of **Skirl Naked** to the lovely ★★ **Harthope Valley** southwest of the town. This valley, formed by a geological fault and smoothed by Ice Age

Jedburgh Abbey

The Border Hotel in Kirk Yetholm

21

Harthope Valley

glaciers, drives 4 miles (6.5 km) straight into the heart of the Cheviots to the tiny hamlet of **Langleeford** at its head, with fine views all around. There is parking at **Carey Burn Bridge** and **Hawsen Burn**. Twelve miles (19km) of footpaths link the valley to The Cheviot and conical Hedgehope Hill to the south – one of the finest viewpoints in the Cheviots. In addition, there are many signposted and waymarked circular walks of various lengths and difficulties leading from the valley, including the 4-mile (6.5km) walk to **Housey Crag** – perhaps the most famous tor in the Cheviots – from lonely **Langlee Cottage**.

High above Langleeford

Also while in Wooler, enquire about a permit (available on a strictly limited basis from John Sale and Partners in Glendale Road) for access to the beautiful ★★ **College Valley** from **Hethpool** and into the very heart of the Cheviots. From Hethpool, a narrow, single-track road takes you 3 miles (5km) south into the valley, where there is limited parking at the shepherd's bungalow of **Mounthooly**. It is a stiff, 8-mile (13km) round walk from here – recommended only for experienced hillwalkers – to the summit of **The Cheviot** (2,676ft/815m) via the dramatic gorge of the **Hen Hole** or **Auchope Cairn** and the **Pennine Way**. A somewhat easier walk is to reach the rocky summit of **The Schil** (1,985ft/605m) which rises to the right via the pass of **Red Cribs** at the head of the valley.

From Wooler, drive east on the B6348 to **Chatton**, where a minor road on the right leads to the Tudor-style estate village of **Chillingham** and ★ **Chillingham Castle** (1 May to 1 October, daily except Tuesdays noon– 5pm; July and August, noon–5.30pm). Chillingham Castle was originally a medieval fortress built in 1245 by the Percys of Alnwick, and both Henry III and Edward III were entertained here. It passed to Sir Thomas Grey, who gave it much of its present appearance in his 1344 reconstruction. In its chequered history it has undergone fires and abandonment, until it was finally restored to its present condition in the 1980s by Sir Humphrey Wakefield.

Chillingham's pride

But Chillingham is perhaps most famous for its herd of ★★ **Wild White Cattle**, which have been left to their own devices since Chillingham Park was first walled in 1220. These magnificent animals, with their black noses and tips to their sweeping horns, are thought by many to be the direct descendants of the aurochs, or extinct wild oxen of Europe, which roamed these islands long before the dawn of history.

Continue to the village of Old Berwick and turn left at the junction with the B6346 to pass through **Harehope** and **Edlingham** and around the grounds of **Hulne Park**, which includes the 13th-century ruins of ★ **Hulne Priory**, to arrive back in **Alnwick**.

Route 2

Coastline and Castles

*Embleton Bay with
Dunstanburgh Castle*

Alnwick – Alnmouth – Warkworth – Craster – Dunstanburgh – Seahouses – Bamburgh – Lindisfarne – Berwick (**50 miles/80km**) *See map, pages 14–15*

The Northumberland coast has been shaped as much by its history as by its geology and the ever-present, all-powerful erosive forces of the North Sea. Although it takes in some of Britain's finest unspoilt and least-frequented beaches, it also encompasses a richness of historical interest which is unmatched in the rest of the country. The medieval strongholds of Dunstanburgh, Bamburgh, Warkworth and Lindisfarne still defiantly stand watch over this lovely coastline, as if determined not to let slip their ancient guardianship role. Powerful families, like the Percys of Alnwick and Warkworth and the Armstrongs of Bamburgh, exerted their iron-fisted Feudal rule over coast and countryside from these impressive fortresses.

High summer in Seahouses

Lindisfarne's alternative name of Holy Island is no hollow Tourist Board epithet. This island, cut off from the mainland by the tides twice a day, was the cradle of Christianity in England in the 7th century, after St Aidan and a group of 12 monks arrived from Iona. That flame of Celtic Christianity was later to spread through the whole of Britain and across Europe. Aidan's successor, St Cuthbert, was to become Northumbria's favourite saint, known as 'the Fire of the North' (*see Culture, page 63*).

The Northumberland Coast Area of Outstanding Natural Beauty (AONB) was designated in 1958 and covers 52 square miles (135 sq. km) north from Amble-by-the-Sea to Berwick-upon-Tweed. It also includes the National Nature Reserve of Lindisfarne, and the protected seabird

Peaceful Alnmouth

sanctuary of the rocky Farne Islands. One of the best-kept secrets of Northumbria is the miles of golden, sandy beaches at places like Alnmouth, Budle and Embleton Bay. Backed by extensive systems of sand dunes, they are among the least spoilt and least visited in Britain.

This 80-mile route takes in the whole of the magnificent Northumberland Coast AONB from Amble to Berwick, allowing time to visit the wonderful collection of castles and fishing villages en route.

Starting from **Alnwick** (*see Route 1*) take the A1068 east to ★ **Alnmouth**, the main seaport for Alnwick in medieval times. Standing on its estuary behind the broad sandy sweep of Alnmouth Bay, Alnmouth was a planned township and some of the tall grain warehouses which handled Northumberland's corn in the 18th century have been tastefully converted into houses and hotels. It is now a peaceful holiday resort.

From Alnmouth, continue south on the A1068 coast road to the pleasant little township of **Warkworth**, standing on a huge loop of the River Coquet. Warkworth is dominated by its magnificent ★★★ **Castle** (English Heritage; 22 March to 31 October, daily 10am–6pm; 1 November to 21 March, 10am–4pm; closed 1–2pm in winter). Originally built in the 11th century, the motte mound at the centre is now dominated by the imposing eight-tower keep – one of the finest in Britain. The unusual slender central watchtower commands spectacular views across Alnmouth Bay.

Warkworth Castle

This was the ancestral home of the Percys who lived here rather than Alnwick until the 16th century. They included Harry Hotspur (Sir Henry Percy) who was brought up here during the 15th century. Shakespeare set three scenes of his *Henry IV* at Warkworth, describing it rather unkindly as 'this worm-eaten hold of ragged stone'. The Duke of Northumberland partly restored the keep in the 19th century and it remains today, in the words of English Heritage, 'an outstanding example of an aristocratic fortified house'.

Warkworth's ★ **Parish Church of St Lawrence** stands at the opposite end to the castle in broad Castle Street, at the apex of the loop in the River Coquet. It has a rare (for Northumbria) spire dating from the 14th century, but inside the church is almost entirely Norman, with a wide chancel arch and unusual stone-vaulted chancel, both built in the 12th century.

A one-mile (1.5km) walk upstream from the village, reached by a short ferry trip across the river, is the romantic ★ **Hermitage** (English Heritage, 1 April to 30 September, Wednesday, Sunday and Bank Holidays 11am–5pm). This hermit's cell hewn from the sandstone cliff probably dates

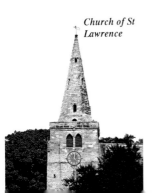

Church of St Lawrence

from the 14th century and is reached by a flight of steps also cut from the living rock. Inside it has a vaulted ceiling and carved scenes from the Passion.

★ **Amble-by-the-Sea** to the south, at the mouth of the Coquet, was once an important coal port. Since the demise of the coal industry in Northumbria, it has developed into a holiday resort, with trips to lighthouse-crowned Coquet Island, and is convenient for the lovely sands of the Druridge Bay Country Park to the south.

Amble-by-the-Sea

From Warkworth, the route returns north on the A1068, and at the roundabout junction to Alnmouth, takes the B1339 coast road through **Lesbury** (sharp left-hand turn) to **Longhoughton**. Take the minor road second right after Longhoughton, to dramatically drop down into the picturesque fishing village of ★★★ **Craster**, famous for its traditionally oak-smoked herrings, better-known as kippers. In addition to the kippers, you can enjoy other fresh fish, crabs, and lobsters in ★ **Robson's Restaurant**, run by a family which have been curing herrings here for four generations.

From Craster harbour, take the easy 1½-mile (2.5km) coastal footpath to the dramatic and isolated ruins of ★★★ **Dunstanburgh Castle** (English Heritage, 22 March to 31 October, daily 10am–6pm; 1 November to 21 March, Wednesday to Sunday 10am–4pm; closed 1–2pm in winter). Note: there is no road access to the castle.

Situated on a 100-ft (30m) high black basalt crag rising from the sea, Dunstanburgh is one of the most evocative and romantically-sited ruins in Britain. Built in 1314 by Thomas, Earl of Lancaster, it was once protected on all sides by the sea using the device of a sea-filled moat on its landward side. In area, Dunstanburgh is the largest of Northumbria's castles, covering 11 acres (4.5 hectares).

Dunstanburgh Castle

25

Morning post, Craster harbour

The most impressive and largest of the surviving fragments is Thomas's great gatehouse, turned into a keep by John of Gaunt in the 1380s.

To the north of the castle lies the magnificent dune-backed sweep of ★★ **Embleton Bay**, which can be reached either by continuing on foot or by returning to Craster and following the minor road through Dunstan to Embleton, where a narrow lane leads to parking by the golf course. Despite its fine sandy beach and the staggeringly beautiful backdrop of the castle, Embleton Bay is seldom very crowded.

The B1339 leads northwards to Beadnell and the busy little harbour town of ★ **Seahouses**. From the harbour you can take an exciting boat trip to the ★★★ **Farne Islands** in season (Inner Farne and Staple Island, the only ones where landing is permitted, are owned by the National Trust and open 28 March to 30 April and 1 August to 30 September, daily 10.30am–6pm). Boat trips to the Farne Islands are run by **Billy Shiel's Boat Trips** or **Mackay's Boat Trips** (both daily, 1 April to 31 October, first sailings 10am, weather permitting; tel: 01665 720308 or 01665 721006).

The 28 Farne Islands are low-lying rocky outcrops of the Whin Sill, famous for their breeding colonies of 55,000 pairs of 21 species of seabirds and their large colony of grey seals, all of which are visible from the boat trips. Inner Farne was used by St Cuthbert as a retreat from 676 to 685, but the present church dates from 1370, and has 17th-century woodwork from Cuthbert's last resting place at Durham Cathedral. Beyond Staple Island is the squat, red-and-white tower of the Longstone Lighthouse, from where Grace Darling set out on her epic rescue mission in 1838. This 23-year-old daughter of the lighthouse keeper spotted the 400-ton passenger steamer *Forfarshire* aground on Big Harcar Rocks, about half a mile to the west, during a fierce northerly gale just before dawn on 7 September, 1838. She raised the alarm, and with her father, launched the tiny coble out into the mountainous seas to save the lives of nine people stranded on the rocks. Grace Darling immediately became a national heroine, but died of consumption just four years later.

From Seahouses, take the B1340 north along the dune-lined coast, where the dramatic outline of Bamburgh beckons. ★★★ **Bamburgh Castle** (1 April to 26 October, daily 11am–5pm) will be familiar to many visitors because its apparently intact medieval profile has so often featured as a backdrop to feature films and movies. Bamburgh has been a stronghold for the local aristocracy since an Iron Age hillfort was the first to utilise the rocky crag of Whin

Bon voyage for the Farne Islands

Farne Islands launch

Bamburgh beckons

Bamburgh Castle

Sill basalt, and the Saxon Queen Bebba, wife of King Ethelfrith, gave the settlement its name – *Bebba's burgh*. The great four-square keep of the castle was built by the Normans in the 1150s, and the building was gradually added to over the centuries. The final restoration, which makes the castle look so misleadingly complete, was executed by Lord Armstrong of Cragside in the late 19th and early 20th centuries. The abiding impression gained from a tour of the rooms is of the heavy-handed Victorian restoration, but the fine collection of armour from the Tower of London is outstanding. Seen from the glorious sands and nature reserve of ★★ **Budle Bay** to the north, Bamburgh remains the most impressive of the Northumberland coastal castles.

27

Tourists in town

The attractive two-street village of Bamburgh nestles beneath the towering red sandstone walls of the castle. Along Radcliffe Road, the ★ **Parish Church of St Aidan** occupies a coastal setting and has a Saxon foundation, but it is most famous for the ostentatious and extravagant vaulted grave of Grace Darling (*see page 26*) in the churchyard. Opposite the church is a small ★ **Grace Darling Museum** (Easter to 30 September and October half-term week, daily 10am–5pm) devoted to the story of Grace, who was born in the village, and her epic rescue, including the original coble boat that she and her father used.

The tomb of Grace Darling

Continuing up the coast, take the B1342, crossing the main east coast railway line before turning right onto the A1 trunk road at **Easington**. After about 6 miles (10km), turn right onto the minor road crossing the railway again through **Beal** towards Holy Island.
N.B. Before crossing on the causeway to Holy Island, check the tide tables at the roadside and take note of the warning signs. Although there is a refuge halfway across, it is better to be safe than sorry.

Lindisfarne Priory

Mead, fudge and honey

The bay and castle

★★★ **Holy Island** or **Lindisfarne** is one of the great holy places of Britain, imbued with an almost tangible sense of spirituality thanks to its place as one of the birthplaces of Celtic Christianity in Britain and Europe (*see Culture, page 63*). It was here that St Aidan came with 12 colleagues from Iona in 635 at the invitation of King Oswald of Bamburgh, just down the coast. Aidan founded the first monastic community on the island, but St Cuthbert extended its influence across the whole of the north of England and beyond.

The romantic remains of ★★★ **Lindisfarne Priory** (English Heritage; 22 March to 31 October, daily 10am–6pm; 1 November to 21 March, 10am–4pm) date from the Benedictine foundation by the Bishop of Durham in 1083. The soft, weathered rose-red sandstone is decorated with many of the carved details found on the columns of Durham Cathedral, and the magnificent 'Rainbow Arch' of the chancel crossing exerts a powerful and beautiful image. Tickets for the priory are purchased at the adjacent **museum**, which displays Saxon carvings from the site in a most lively and entertaining way. Adjoining the priory is the orginally-12th century **St Mary's Parish Church**, which contains copies of the Lindisfarne Gospels (original in the British Museum).

★★ **Lindisfarne Village** is an odd mixture of traditional buildings and modern bungalows. An architecturally nondescript building contains **St Aidan's Winery** (8 January to end September, daily according to crossing times; 1 October to 21 December, Monday to Friday according to crossing times), the home of the famous Lindisfarne Mead, fudge and preserves.

★★ **Lindisfarne Castle** (National Trust; 28 March to 30 October, daily except Friday 1–5.30pm, according to crossing times) on Beblowe Crag at the south-eastern ex-

tremity of the 1,350-acre (546 hectare) island is a bit of a sham. Originally built as a fort in 1550 to protect Henry VIII's fleet, it was largely rebuilt in romantic, medieval style by the architect Sir Edward Lutyens for the owner Edward Hudson, founder of *Country Life* magazine. It shows Lutyens at his most inventive, with rooms hollowed out of walls and a fine collection of oak furniture. The tiny walled garden is by Gertrude Jeykyll.

The island itself is worth a longer exploration on foot, from the upturned herring boats serving as sheds on the bay front near the castle, to the adjacent lime kilns and lovely pebble beaches of Emmanuel Head, and the long sand and shingle neck leading to the sandy beaches and dunes of The Snook. Lindisfarne is a National Nature Reserve, famed for its bird and plant communities, which include eiders ('Cuddy's Ducks'), scoters and puffins, as well as an important over-wintering population of whooper swans and Brent geese on The Slakes mudflats between the island and the mainland.

Berwick-upon-Tweed

29

Return to the A1 and turn right (north) for 8 miles (13km) to enter ★★ **Berwick-upon-Tweed**, an ancient town which has alternated its allegiances between England and Scotland 11 times since it was first surrendered to the English in 1174. It legally became part of Northumberland as late as 1974. Architecturally, the most impressive feature of Berwick are its almost perfectly intact Elizabethan ★★★ **Walls and Ramparts** (English Heritage, open any reasonable time), built between 1558 and 1569 when the Scots and French invasion threat was at its height. A walk around them, perhaps taking in the elegant 18th-century Vanbrugh-designed ★★ **Barracks** (English Heritage; 22 March to 31 October, daily 10am–6pm; 1 November to 21 March, Wednesday to Sunday 10am–4pm; closed 1–2pm in winter), the Georgian ★★ **Main Guard House** (English Heritage, managed by the Berwick Civic Society; 28–31 March, 3–5 May, 24–26 May and 1 June to 30 September, daily except Wednesday 1–5pm), and the ruins of the 12th-century ★ **Castle** (English Heritage; open any reasonable time), should not be missed.

The Ramparts

In this town of outstanding architecture, Berwick's ★★ **Parish Church of the Holy Trinity** is especially interesting because it was entirely built during the Commonwealth period (1648–52). Among Berwick's other landmarks are the column-fronted 18th-century **Guildhall**, and its bridges across the rushing salmon-rich Tweed. The massive, 388-yard (355m) **Old Bridge** was built in 1603 and remained the only road bridge until the **Royal Tweed Bridge** was built in 1928. Built between the two, Robert Stephenson's 28-arch **Royal Border Bridge** was built to carry the railway in 1846.

Route 3

The Simonside Hills

Rothbury – Lordenshaws – Forestburn Gate – Wallington – Elsdon – Rothbury (20 miles/32 kms) *See map, pages 14–15*

Simonside resident

Lordenshaws fort and the Simonside Ridge

Lordenshaws: a close inspection

Like a little piece of the Pennines stranded between the Cheviots and the sea, the Simonside Hills, blanketed on their northern slopes by the bottle-brush conifers of Rothbury Forest, present a dramatic 5-mile (8km) ridge rising above the valley of Coquetdale between Elsdon and Rothbury. Laid down during the Carboniferous period about 350 million years ago, the Fell Sandstones which form these hills stretch in a wide arc of steep crags with heather-covered scarp slopes behind. The views northward from the escarpment towards the distant, misty shapes of the Cheviots on the horizon are among the finest in Northumberland.

The Simonside Ridge rises to 1,443ft (440m) at Tosson Hill, and includes the eponymous summit of Simonside (1,407ft/428m), which is thought to take its name from the Scandinavian *Sigemund's Seat*, known as *Simundesette* in 1279, *sett* being the Old English word for settlement or dwelling place. The open moorland of Lordenshaws and Garleigh Moor to the northeast of the ridge, apparently empty now, epitomises the palimpsest which is the Northumbrian landscape. Layer upon layer of history has been imprinted on the heather and rank grass of this now deserted moor.

This shorter half-day route encircles the Simonside Hills, taking in not only some exceptional scenery but also a fine country house.

Leave Rothbury heading south on the B6342, climbing out of Coquetdale across a shoulder of the Simonside Hills which rise to the right. After about 3 miles (5km), a minor road (signed 'Simonside') leads right towards the important prehistoric landscape of ★★★ **Lordenshaws**.

The most prominent feature just north of the car park is the large circular double banks and ditches of the Lordenshaws **Iron Age hillfort**, which was built around 350BC. It commands outstanding views to the north across the roofs of Rothbury and the valley of the Coquet towards the distant Cheviots. Northeast of the fort, large cairns of stones mark Bronze Age burial mounds. In one, the open stone grave or 'cist' is exposed, where the body of the deceased once crouched.

All around the fort the corrugations of the **rig and furrow** produced by ploughing by oxen teams during the Middle Ages can be seen. Crossing the area from north to south is the **boundary bank** and wall of the 13th-century deer park of the Royal Forest of Rothbury (*see* Forestburn Gate below).

A grass path to the west of the fort leads to a large sandstone boulder outcrop on the surface. This is one of the most interesting **carved rocks** at Lordenshaws: closer inspection will reveal the earliest visible remains of prehistoric man in the area – the enigmatic 'cup and ring' marks of concentric circles, interlinking channels and deep circular cups. No one is certain of the meaning of these intricate carvings, which are thought to date from the Neolithic period and are probably about 5,000 years old, but it has been suggested that the distribution of these and similar carvings found elsewhere indicates that they may be associated with ancient trackways and particular viewpoints, providing messages of some kind to people passing through the area. Whatever its origins and function, the Lordenshaw collection of 'rock art' is one of the finest in the North of England.

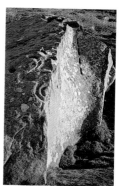

Lordenshaws:
cup and ring detail

31

The car park at Lordenshaws is also a convenient starting point for one of the finest walking excursions in Northumbria, an 8-mile (13-km) roller-coaster route west along the Simsonside Ridge over **Dove Crag**, **Simonside** (1,407ft/428m) and **Raven's Heugh**, with outstanding views north across Coquetdale to the Cheviots at every step. Return via the forestry tracks through the conifers of Rothbury Forest at the foot of the ridge.

Hiking on the Simonside Ridge

Back on the B6342, continue south on the moorland road on the edge of the hills through the village of **Forestburn Gate**. The name of the village relates to an entrance to the ancient Royal Hunting Forest of Rothbury, owned by the Crown from the 11th to 13th centuries. Medieval kings hunted wild boar, deer and probably wolves in this enclosed area, and the remains of the later 13th-century walls of the deer park can still be seen on the hills. By the mid-14th century, the forest had passed to the famous Border family of the Percys whose heirs, the Dukes of Northumberland, still own the land.

The road continues south, crossing a high point of 840ft (256m) before descending steeply to cross the Font Burn where it flows from the outlet from the **Fontburn Reservoir** which nestles in a fold of the hills to the right. The road now zigzags up out of the Font Burn valley and across the moors, with the Simonside Hills still rising away to the right. Descending now, the route crosses the eastern arm of **Rothley Lakes**, another reservoir, before turning sharply right (west).

Wallington: the Central Hall

At the next sharp bend in the road, ignore for the moment the minor road signposted to Elsdon, continuing along the B6342 for 4 miles (7km) further south through the village of **Cambo**, where the famous 17th-century landscape gardener Launcelot 'Capability' Brown was educated, to ★★★ **Wallington House** (National Trust; house: 28 March to end of September daily except Tuesday 1–5.30pm, last admission 5pm; 1 October to 2 November 1–4.30pm, last admission 4pm; grounds: all year from 10am during daylight hours). Built in 1688 on the site of a medieval castle, Wallington is the family home of the Trevelyan family. The finely-decorated rooms range from Georgian to mid-Victorian, and the 19th-century Central Hall has a fine collection of paintings of 'Scenes from Northumbrian History' by the pre-Raphaelite painter William Bell Scott. Children will love the doll's house collection, and the period Children's Room. There is an enchanting terraced **walled garden** with themed mixed borders, and don't miss the impressive 'Wallington Beasts', a much-photographed collection of four mythical oriental dragons' heads occupying a space near the ha-ha wall at the edge of the house's main lawn.

Wallington Beasts and the walled garden

Back on the minor road off the B6342, the route now leads west for 7 miles (11km) along the edge of the dark, monotonous conifers of the modern Harwood Forest, which has cloaked the southern slopes of the Simonsides in a blanket of alien Sitka spruce trees. About 4 miles (6.5km) on, as the road starts to drop down towards **Elsdon** (*see Route 1*), there are fine views of the village and northeastwards along the ridge of the Simonside Hills towards the frowning heights of Dough Crag (1,264ft/385m).

Leave Elsdon on the B6341 past the Norman motte and bailey castle, up over Billsmoor and down into the Grasslees Valley, before returning to Rothbury along the north bank of the Coquet, passing through the villages of **Hepple**, **Flotterton** and **Thropton** (*see Route 1*).

Route 4

Kielder Country

Kielder Country from Blakehope Nick

Bellingham – Kielder Water – Kielder Village – (detour to Hermitage Castle) – Kielder Forest Drive – Black Middens Bastle – Bellingham (40 miles/64km) *See map, pages 14–15*

33

In its own, totally-artificial way, Kielder is a unique landscape. It represents the largest man-made lake in Europe surrounded by the largest planted forest in Europe – an entirely unnatural yet not always unattractive landscape. It is an extremely popular place for recreation, especially for visitors from nearby Tyneside. The miles of forest rides and tracks are very popular with walkers and mountain bikers, and there are many opportunities for water sports on the huge, 2,684-acre (1,085 hectare) reservoir itself.

Log jam in Kielder

The generic name of Kielder Forest includes the forestry blocks of Kielder, Wark, Falstone and Redesdale and covers about 300 sq. miles (777 sq. km) of former moorland in mainly alien conifers. The first purchases by the Forestry Commission were made soon after its formation in the early 1920s, for planting as a 'strategic reserve' of timber against possible future national emergencies such as another World War. In 1932, 47,000 acres (19,000 hectares) of what is now the nucleus of Kielder Forest were purchased from the Duke of Northumberland, and land continued to be bought and planted until 1969.

The most common tree species in the forests are Sitka spruce, Norway spruce, Lodgepole pine and Japanese larch, but on the drier, heathery knolls in the forest, the native Scots pine is also planted. In today's more enlightened world, the Commission plants many more native, broadleaved trees for their conservation value and as habi-

Fishing on Kielder Water

tats for wildlife, because the alien conifers are of relatively poor value. There are over 500 miles (800km) of forest roads in Kielder Forest, and some of these are open to the public as forest drives. Others are used for horse-riding and as off-road cycling routes.

Kielder Water reservoir, opened in 1982, was constructed to meet the predicted – but largely unfulfilled – demand for water from the cities of Tyneside and Teesside into the 21st century. It was a controversial development, and although the demand for industrial use never materialised to the extent which was expected, Northumbrian Water has been able in recent years to 'export' water from Kielder to the drought-stricken water companies further south in the Pennines.

This 40-mile (64km) circular drive from Bellingham is an easy day's outing, and provides many opportunities for stopping and exploring the popular southern shores of Kielder Water and its surrounding forests. It continues by taking the unsurfaced Forest Drive from Kielder Castle to Bryness, returning through Redesdale to Bellingham. A 50-mile (80km) detour to the west from Kielder takes in the imposing Border stronghold of Hermitage Castle, across the Scottish Border.

Bellingham

★★ **Bellingham** (pronounced 'Bellin-jam') is a welcome landmark on the Pennine Way and a pleasant, small market town founded on former iron and coal workings, which serves as the 'Gateway to Kielder' for many visitors. It is the chief town of North Tynedale and its wide main street leads south to the small, towerless ★★ **Parish Church of St Cuthbert**, which has a fine, barrel-vaulted 13th-century chancel, remodelled in the early 17th century. The original church on this site was frequently torched during the troubled times of the Border wars, so was rebuilt with a remarkable roof of heavy stone slabs supported in the nave and transept by 22 massive transverse stone arches. ★ **Bellingham Heritage Centre**, at Shellcroft in Front Street (May to September, Friday to Monday 10.30am– 5.30pm, plus Easter weekend) has changing exhibitions on Border life, including special features on the Border Counties Railway, local churches and the reivers.

Take the minor road signposted 'Kielder' west from Bellingham, passing up the valley of the River North Tyne for about 9 miles (15km) through Hesleyside and Stannersburn to reach the eastern end of Kielder Water near **Falstone**. ★★★ **Kielder Water** has a 27-mile (43km) shoreline, and a good starting point for its exploration is on the right just past Falstone – the ★★ **Tower Knowe Visitor Centre** (April and October, daily 10am–4pm; May to September 10am–5pm; November to March 10am–4pm). The centre is run jointly by Northumbrian Water and the Northumberland National Park, and has a fascinating interpretive display as well as a gift shop. There is a short self-guided trail from the Visitor Centre which takes you along the lake shore to the remains of a Romano-British settlement, now partly submerged.

Continue on the minor road west from Tower Knowe, which climbs up past **Elf Kirk Quarry** (left) with fine ★ **views** across the southern reaches of Kielder Water. The road now descends through the forestry and round the bay of Whickhope, where ★ **Kielder Water Cruises** (1 April to 30 September, daily 11am–3.30pm; tel. 01434 240398) offer 75-minute cruises in an 80-seat boat complete with heated lounge and light refreshments.

The road now turns north through the conifers past many tempting picnic sites. After another mile on the right you pass the ★ **Leaplish Waterside Park** (May to September, daily 10am–5pm; October to April, 10am–4pm), which provides water sports, fishing, log cabins, a caravan site, cycle hire, a restaurant, sauna and solarium. There are good views of the reservoir from the **Beeches Promontory Car Park**.

Leaplish Waterside Park

35

Continue north for another 3 miles (5km), as Kielder Water eventually gives way to its smaller, northern extension, the ★★ **Bakethin Reservoir** on the right. There is a self-guided Nature Trail around the more intimate northern shores of the reservoir, which leads to the mighty ★ **Kielder Viaduct**, a splendid 'skew' viaduct built in 1862 as part of the former Border Counties Railway, which ran from Hexham up the North Tyne Valley.

Hikers at Bakethin Reservoir

It is now less than a mile to **Kielder Village**, a 1950s forestry village, which is now the headquarters of the Forestry Commission's Border Forest operations, based in the late 18th-century castellated shooting lodge of the Duke of Northumberland, **Kielder Castle**. The ★★ **Visitor Centre** in the castle (28 March to 31 October, daily 10am–5pm; August 10am–6pm; 1 January to 27 March, November and December, weekends only 11am–4pm) has an interesting interpretive display on local history.

Kielder Viaduct

From Kielder Castle, it is possible to make a detour across the Scottish Border to visit one of the most forbidding of the Border fortresses. Continue northwest to cross the border at **Deadwater**, then descend into Liddesdale, a former reiver stronghold, via **Saughtree**, where you turn left onto the B6357 through **Larriston** and **Old Castleton** towards **Newcastleton**. Turn right onto the B6399, and just before the village of Hermitage, a minor road on the left leads to ★★★ **Hermitage Castle** (Historic Scotland; 1 April to 30 September, Monday to Saturday 9.30am–6pm,

Hermitage Castle and Bothwell

Kielder Burn

Black Middens: the stairs

Sunday 2–6pm; closed October to March). The roofless castle, once known as 'the strength of Liddesdale', dates from the 14th century, and has been held successively by the great Border families of Soulis, Dacre, Douglas and Bothwell. The most famous event in the castle's history took place when the fourth Earl of Bothwell was visited here in 1566 by Mary Queen of Scots, as he recovered from a wound sustained in a border skirmish. Mary was still married to Lord Darnley, so the tryst could only be a short one. But Darnley was murdered only four months later and Bothwell, implicated in the murder, duly became Mary's third husband. Hermitage was Sir Walter Scott's favourite castle, and the grim, towering, corbelled walls always seem to exert a threatening, mournful atmosphere.

From Hermitage, either return the way you came or follow the B6399 north for 15 miles to **Hawick** and then southeast on the A6088 to Carter Bar, returning to the main route and Bellingham via the A68.

Back in Kielder Village, follow the tolled ★★ **Forest Drive** which leads northeast eventually to emerge from the claustrophobic conifers on the banks of the Kielder Burn at Hall Knowe and the pleasantly-situated **Kielder Burn Picnic Site**. Follow the Forest Drive signs on the now unsurfaced road which leads past East Kielder Farm and into the valley of the Ridge End Burn. The road climbs eastwards through the stifling blanket of conifers which covers Ewe Hill and East Kielder Moor, escaping from the trees at **Blakehope Nick**, the highest point of the drive at 1,489ft (454m). The strangely named **Oh Me Edge** (1,809ft/551m) lies across the moorland to the left and **Berrymoor Edge** (1,505ft/459m) is the high point looking right. The forest drive now plunges back down into the conifers of **Redesdale Forest** for another 3 miles (5km) to emerge at the hamlet of **Bakehopeburnhaugh** in Redesdale, which vies with the neighbouring hamlet of **Cottonshopeburnfoot** for the title of the longest English placename.

Turn right here on the A68, passing through Rochester, Horsley and Elishaw (*see Route 1*). A mile beyond Elishaw turn sharp right at a crossroads signposted Bellingham onto the B6320. This leads across the rough, featureless grasslands and moorland of Troughend Common. After about 3 miles (5km), a sign to the right onto a minor road leads through **Gatehouse** to ★★ **Black Middens Bastle House** (English Heritage, open at any reasonable time), one of the best-preserved of the Northumbrian bastles (or defended farmhouses). This solid, two-storey structure with its outside stairs and massive 4-ft (1.2m) thick walls dates from the 16th century and is one of three in the vicinity on the edge of the Tarset Burn.

Return to **Bellingham** in about 7 miles via the B6320.

Route 5

The Wall at Cuddy's Crags

Wall Country

Hexham – Haydon Bridge – Haltwhistle – Lanercost
– Thirlwall – Vindolanda – Housesteads – Chesters –
Hexham **(about 70 miles/112km)** *See map, pages 38–9*

There was once much more to Hadrian's Wall than the 73-mile (117km) long fortifications running across the neck of England. Thriving civilian settlements, known as *vici*, spread out to the south behind the protection of the 16-ft (5m) high Wall. These *vici*, with houses and temples, shops and theatres, not only served the temporal needs of the 10,000 auxilliary soldiers from all over the Empire who were stationed on this last northern outpost of Rome. They also became important trading settlements for the surrounding population of local tribespeople. This dependent civilian settlement based on the Wall is now much better understood, and museums at places like Housesteads, Vindolanda and Birdoswald tell a very different story from the classroom clichés of the Romans fending off constant attacks from the 'Picts and Scots'.

The Hadrian's Wall Military Zone, including many of these associated civilian settlements, was designated a World Heritage by UNESCO in 1987 because of the importance of its cultural and archaeological landsapes, and this 70-mile (100km) circular route from Hexham visits many of the most important sites along the way. A full day should be put aside for this route.

The focal point of the historic market town of **Hexham** (market days: Tuesday and Saturday) is the squat-towered ★★ **Abbey** (May to September, daily 9am–7pm; October to April, 9am–5pm). Originally founded by Wilfrid

Fresh discoveries at Vindolanda

Hexham Abbey

Early English transepts

The Border History Museum

in about 675, it was sacked by Danish raiders a year later and refounded as an Augustinian priory in 1113. The only remaining part of Wilfrid's Saxon church is the ★★ **Crypt**, reached by the steps in the centre of the nave. One of the finest Saxon crypts in England, it was constructed of Roman masonry from the nearby fort of *Corstopitum* (Corbridge). ★ **The Frith Stool**, a tub-shaped stone chair, is said to be Wilfrid's throne, and is also certainly Saxon in style, but perhaps the greatest architectural glory of the Abbey are the beautiful 12th- and 13th-century **Early English transepts**, which on the south side include the unique Night Stair leading down from the former Augustianian canons' dormitory to the central crossing.

Narrow streets lined with some fine Georgian houses radiate from the central **Market Square**, and the whole central part of the town, including the lovely **Abbey Grounds** and **Sele** town park, is now a Conservation Area. The **Tourist Information Centre** is housed in the imposing **Manor Office** in Hallgate – also known as **The Old Gaol** – which houses the ★★ **Border History Museum** (Easter to end of October, daily 10am–4.30pm; February to Easter, Saturday to Tuesday 10am–4.30pm). This lively local museum is housed in what is claimed to be the first purpose-built prison in England (it dates from 1330) and includes displays and audio-visual shows illustrating the Border warfare of the 15th and 16th centuries, as well as the 1715 Jacobite Rebellion.

Take the B6531 out of Hexham, joining the busy A69 Newcastle to Carlisle road on the Hexham by-pass. Turn left (west) towards **Haydon Bridge**, once strategically-important during the Anglo-Scottish wars, when the bridge crossing the Tyne was locked against the Scottish invaders.

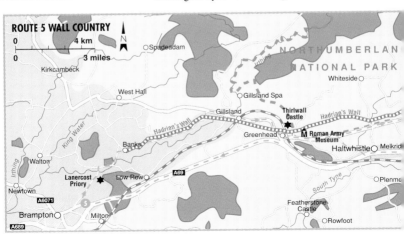

It suffers now from the constant traffic on the A69, which we follow westwards for 9 miles (14km) through Bardon Mill, Henshaw and Melkridge to **Haltwhistle**. Haltwhistle's name (or 'Hautwessel' as it is pronounced by locals) comes from Old English and means 'the junction of streams by the hill'. Like many towns in this area, it suffered from Scottish raids, but the ★ **Church of the Holy Cross**, set on a sloping site in the middle of the town, is worth a visit for its almost entirely 13th-century irregular iron-stained masonry.

Keeping time in Haltwhistle

Our route now swings northwest towards the Wall itself, and signposted about 3 miles (5km) further along the A68 near **Greenhead** is the ★★ **Roman Army Museum** (February to November daily from 10am; closing time varies with season). This exciting museum is adjacent to the unexcavated Roman fort of *Magnis* at Carvoran and is devoted to the life of the Roman soldiers stationed on the Wall. Vivid reconstructions, models and audio-visual programmes bring the past to life.

Continue west on the A69 from Greenhead, paralleling the Wall to the south for 9 miles (16km), and passing Denton Fell to the left and the valley of the River Irthing to your right. About a mile before the busy little market town of **Brampton**, turn right onto a minor road signposted to ★★ **Lanercost Priory** (English Heritage; 22 March to 31 October, daily 10am–6pm), reached in another 2 miles (3km) and beautifully situated in the wooded valley of the Irthing. The original Augustinian priory was founded around 1166 by Robert de Vallibus (or Vaux). Entered through an ancient gatehouse, the elegant Early English nave and north aisle of the priory now serve as the parish church of St Mary Magdalene. The rest of the chancel,

Lanercost Priory

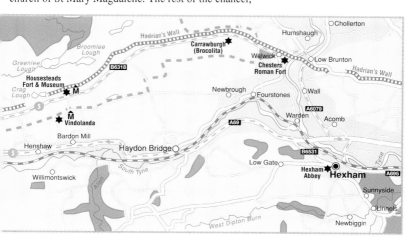

The undercroft at Lanercost

transepts and priory buildings are in ruins, but from the former monastic building known as Dacre Hall, steps lead down to the vaulted **13th-century undercroft**, which has been likened to a mini version of the Cellarium at the much more famous Fountain's Abbey in Yorkshire.

Follow the minor road east from Lanercost to cross the vallum of the Wall at the significantly-named **Banks** to reach the B6318. Turn right through **Gisland** and just before Greenhead, at the other side of the railway line and high above the Tipalt Burn on the Pennine Way, stands the ruined 14th-century pele tower of ★ **Thirlwall Castle** (private), built with masonry from the Wall by the de Thirlwall family. This is a good place to explore the Wall on foot, as it crosses the whinstone ridge known as the Nine Nicks of Thirlwall.

From here, the B6318 follows the line of the Roman **Stanegate**, the military road which served the south side of the Wall. Passing the Roman Army Museum again, the route now shadows the Wall across Haltwhistle Common alongside its most exciting and scenic section.

Exploring Vindolanda

After about 7 miles (11km), signs lead off to the right to Chesterholm Roman Fort at ★★★ **Vindolanda** (February to November daily from 10am). This is a must for any Wall enthusiast, because it is the only place where full-size reconstructions of the Wall and a turret can be seen reaching to their original height, giving a real impression of the sheer, overwhelming scale of Hadrian's enterprise. A stretch of earlier turf wall with a milecastle gate has also been reconstructed by the charitable trust which runs the site. There is also a replica Roman temple, house and shop, and a large open-air museum which is set in lovely gardens. But perhaps the most touching exhibits in the museum are the rare fragments of wooden writing tablets and artefacts like shoes and pieces of cloth which record everyday life on the Wall.

Back on the B6318, it is a short distance to the most impressively situated remains of the original Wall and the best preserved major fort at ★★★ **Housesteads Fort and Museum** (English Heritage/National Trust/Northumberland National Park; 1 April to 30 September, daily 10am–6pm; 1 October to 31 March, daily 10am–4pm). Housesteads (*Vercovicium*) is easily the most impressive Roman fort on the Wall, built around AD128 in typical playing-card shape and 5 acres (2 hectares) in extent. In the early days, up to 1,000 infantry soldiers were garrisoned here, later to be reinforced by cavalry. Most of the extensive remains visible today date from the 3rd and 4th centuries, and they include a headquarters building, the commanding officer's house, barracks, bath houses, latrines, workshops, a hospital and a granary.

The granary at Housesteads

As you walk up to the fort from the road, you pass through the bumps and hollows of the terraces of the extensive Roman civil settlement (or *vicus*) which existed outside the walls. Away to the left is the barn which serves as joint **National Trust/National Park Visitor Centre**.

After exploring the astonishingly complete remains of the fort, it is worth taking a short stroll beside the Wall to the west, up through the straggling pines which cap Cuddy's (Cuthbert's) and Hotbank Crags on one of the finest stretches of the Wall for the walker. Looking north from the crags of the Great Whin Sill above the deep, glacial lake of **Crag Lough** gives a vivid impression of what it must have been like for the Roman soliders posted to this remote northernmost outpost of the Empire.

Modern poses near Crag Lough

Continuing east on the B6318, the route still sticks to the Wall and Vallum, past the fort of ★ **Carrawburgh** (*Brocolita*) with its Mithraic Temple and Shrine to Coventina, before bearing right and dropping down into the valley of the North Tyne again at **Chesters**, where you can still see the extensive remains of the abutments of the Roman bridge on which the Wall crossed the river.

★★ **Chesters Roman Fort** (English Heritage; 22 March to 31 October, daily 9.30am–6pm or dusk in October; 1 November to 21 March, daily 10am–4pm) or *Cilurnum* was built to defend the bridgehead in the 2nd century and housed about 500 calvalrymen. The site museum is one of the most interesting on the Wall, and includes several important Roman sculptures, altars and inscriptions, many of which were the result of finds by the archaeologist John Clayton, owner of the fort site in 1832. The remains include the finest military bath house in Britain.

From Chesters, take the A6079 south for 3 miles (5km) and back into **Hexham**.

Roman pose at Brocolita

Crag Lough

Durham and the River Wear

Route 6

Durham City Walk

Monkeys in the market place

Durham Cathedral and Castle were designated as one of the first World Heritage Sites in Britain by UNESCO in 1987. The honour gave formal recognition to what many believe is the finest Norman Gothic cathedral and close in Europe. The unique cultural grouping of the city's finest buildings is matched by their spectacular natural setting, on an island peninsula formed by a loop of the River Wear.

The Saxon name *Dunholm* perfectly describes the site of the historic core of the city, and literally means 'hill island'. It also reflects the chequered cultural history of Durham and Northumbria, *Dun* coming from the Old English, meaning hill, and *holm* from the Scandinavian *holmr*, meaning island. The first settlement of Durham was probably during the Stone Age, but the first visible prehistoric remains comprise the Iron Age hillfort of Maiden Castle, on a slight hill once moated on three sides by the River Wear to the east of the present city. The area below the fort is now used as playing fields by the University of Durham. Nearby is the hamlet of Old Durham, where a settlement of the same period has been identified.

The present city owes its foundation to Northumbria's favourite saint, Cuthbert, who was finally laid to rest on the wooded, rocky peninsula in 995 by the last in a succession of monks who had been carrying his body around the north for about 120 years, attempting to avoid the then frequent Viking raids. A popular legend states that by the end of the 990s the Viking raids had eased, and the loyal monks decided to return Cuthbert's body to Lindisfarne. As they approached the great loop in the River Wear where Durham now stands, Cuthbert's coffin became impossibly heavy to lift. One monk had a vision in which Cuthbert said he wanted to be buried at 'Dunholme', but no one knew where Dunholme was. As they pondered on what to do, they overheard two peasant women, one of whom had lost her cow on Dunholme. As they started to follow the women up the wooded slope, Cuthbert's coffin miraculously became easy to carry – and they knew they had found his proper resting place. If you look carefully at a niche carved in the eastern turret of the cathedral overlooking Dun Cow Lane, you will see the two women of the legend with their cow.

The present cathedral replaced the original wooden 'White Church' built by the monks and was started in 1093 by Bishop William and largely completed by 1189. It is widely regarded as the finest example of Early Norman architecture in Britain, and one of the greatest Romanesque cathedrals in the world. The castle – now part of the University of Durham – was begun just 20 years before the present cathedral. Built to protect the narrow neck of the peninsula on its northern side, it was until the 19th century the seat of the all-powerful Prince Bishops of Durham.

Seat of the Prince Bishops

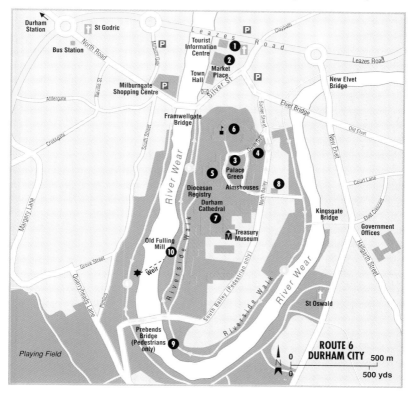

ROUTE 6
DURHAM CITY

This short walk around the great Durham peninsula takes in most of the wonderful buildings of the city, but you should allow a full day for a proper exploration of this most complete and beautiful of English cathedral cities.

Start from the **Market Place** which is situated on the 'neck' of the Durham peninsula. The **Tourist Information Centre** (July to August daily; September to June, Monday to Saturday) is centrally placed in the corner of the Market Place, near ★ **St Nicholas's Church ❶**, originally built in the 12th century but almost entirely rebuilt in 1858. In the 14th century, its north wall formed part of the city walls. To the left of the TIC is the ★ **Guildhall ❷**, with its Tudur arched doors and balcony and adjacent **Town Hall** – the civic centrepieces of the city. The Guildhall (closed weekends) was originally built in 1356 by Bishop Tunstall and rebuilt in 1665 by Bishop Cosin. It was entirely rebuilt in 1851 in Perpendicular Tudor style as part of a new Town Hall and Market complex.

The copper-plated equestrian statue in the centre of the Market Place depicts the 3rd Marquis of Londonderry and was erected in 1861, while the **statue of Neptune** on the Pant, or well-head, was returned to its rightful spot in 1991 after removal in 1923.

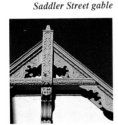

The statue of Neptune

44

Saddler Street gable

Bishop Cosin's Hall

Walk south from the cobbled Market Square and ascend the gentle slope of **Saddler Street** between the varied, mainly Tudor gables, visible above the modern shopfronts. This part of Saddler Street was originally known as Fleshergate after the many butchers, once known as 'flesh-hewers' who traded here. Continue up the street, past the cobbled Magdalen Steps, before turning right into **Owengate**, noting **Halmote Court** on the left, the site of the originally 14th-century manorial court of the city. It was rebuilt in 1850.

After a few more uphill steps, you emerge onto the large expanse of **Palace Green ❸**, and the imposing sight of the full northern aspect of Durham Cathedral in front of you, which in medieval days was obscured by houses and a market. The Green is now just lawn, but ranged around it are some of the finest buildings in Durham, many of which played a vital role in this, the administrative hub of the fabled prince-bishops.

Looking from left to right, almost immediately to the left is the elegant 17th-century red-brick mansion known as **Bishop Cosin's Hall ❹**. The low, gabled building next door is **Bishop Cosin's Almshouses**, built in 1666 to house eight poor people of the city, and which is now a tearoom. To the right of the cathedral, **Windy Gap** – wellnamed for the boisterous winds which sometimes blow up it – is a *vennel* (the local name for an alleyway) leading down to the 17th-century **Grammar School** and the riverside walk along the banks of the Wear. Beyond Windy Gap is the **Diocesan Registry**, which served as Durham's civil county court between 1588 and 1811. The next building to the right is **Bishop Cosin's Library** , the doorway of which is a favourite photographic backdrop for proud students who have just graduated from the Durham University colleges. The library was founded by the great Durham benefactor and bishop in 1669 for the use of both public and clergy. The ancient building next on the right is Bishop Neville's **Exchequer and Chancery**, built around the middle of the 15th century to include his own court and mint for coins.

In the right-hand corner of the Green, a shady, cobbled lane leads through an imposing, turretted gateway into ★★★ **Durham Castle** ❻, now **University College**,

Durham Castle and visitors

Durham (guided tours only: July to end of September, Monday to Saturday 10am–noon and 2–4.30pm, Sunday 2–4.30pm only; otherwise Monday, Wednesday and Saturday, 2–4.30pm. Note that tours may be cancelled when there are university events taking place in the castle).

Durham Castle is one of the largest Norman castles and finest Romanesque palaces in Britain. It was begun in 1072 as a typical motte and bailey. Added to over the years, the greatest rebuilding was by Bishop Hugh of Le Puiset, builder of the Lady Chapel of the cathedral and one of the powerful Prince Bishops of Durham. The Palatinate of Durham was founded by William the Conqueror to quell the threat of Scottish invasion. He chose his Prince Bishops personally, and they were allowed their own parliament, laws, coinage and army in return for their allegiance to the monarch. The jurisdiction of the Prince Bishop was only finally surrendered to the Crown as late as 1836, and a year later, the castle became University College.

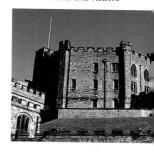

Features of particular interest in the castle, all included in the guided tour, are the partly medieval **Great Hall**, where students from Durham University colleges gather for their graduations, the **Norman Chapel**, and the beautifully carved **Norman doorway**, which owes much in its style to the architecture of the cathedral across the Green.

Walk across the Green to the ★★★ **Cathedral** ❼ (May to August, daily 7.15am–8pm; September to April, 7.15am–6pm), admiring first of all the magnificent 11th-century Devil-faced ★ **Sanctuary Knocker** on the North Door.

Entering the cathedral, the visitor is overwhelmed by the massive, Norman columns which stride down the nave like a petrified forest of stone. Boldly incised with spirals, lozenges, zigzags and flutings, their impact is stunning. Looking up to the majestic ribbed vaulting of the nave, it is worth noting that Durham Cathedral was the first major English church to be entirely covered by a stone

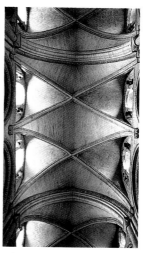

Ribbed vaulting in the cathedral

The Millennium Window

The Cloisters

St Cuthbert's pectoral cross

vault, and one of the earliest in Europe to use ribbed vaulting. The whole impression is one of wonderful strength yet soaring spaciousness.

Of the many outstanding features of this building, mention should be made of the superb ★★★ **Galilee Chapel** (c1170), with its strongly-modelled zigzag ornamentation on its Romanesque arches and the tomb of one of the first English historians, the Venerable Bede (died AD735). It is well worth taking a stroll around the beautiful ★★ **Cloisters** (1388–1405), and at the eastern end of the cathedral, in the ★★★ **Chapel of the Nine Altars** (c1280), lie the remains of **St Cuthbert** under a simple but touching plain black marble slab. Also, in the main cathedral, take time to admire some of the stained glass, including some notable modern works: a stylised depiction of the Last Supper near the north door and, in the south aisle, the superb **Millennium Window**, depicting many aspects of the history and contemporary life of County Durham.

Certainly worth a visit is the cathedral's ★★★ **Treasury Museum** (Monday to Saturday 10am–4.30pm, Sunday 2–4.30pm), which contains among other treasures relics of St Cuthbert, including his wooden coffin and wonderful pectoral cross, plus altar plate, illustrated manuscripts and richly embroidered copes.

Leave the cathedral and turn right to walk down **Dun Cow Lane**, not forgetting to look up at the carving depicting the legend of Cuthbert (*see page 43*) on the eastern turret. This leads down to **North Bailey**, where, almost opposite on the corner of Bow Lane, is the Church of St Mary le Bow, now the ★ **Durham Heritage Centre ❽** (April to 25 May, Saturday and Sunday 2–4.30pm; 26 May to end June and 1–28 September, daily 2–4.30pm; July and August, daily 11.30am–4.30pm). A 12th-century church partly rebuilt in the 17th century, it shows the history of the city through exhibitions and audio-visual displays.

Turn left down North Bailey (which follows the line of the castle's former bailey) back into Saddler Street. Then turn right down **Magdalen Steps** into **Souterpeth** (the shoemakers' street), turning right just before crossing **Elvet Bridge**, which originally dates from the 12th century, to descend onto the ★★ **Riverside Walk**.

You soon enter a pleasant woodland path by the side of the Wear, passing under the sweeping modern shape of **Kingsgate Bridge** (1963), designed by the architect responsible for the Sydney Opera House in Australia, Ove Arup. The southern end of the peninsula shows some of the finest remaining sections of the medieval **Castle Walls**, closely buttressed and towering above the path to the right. Turning the bend in the river, you come to a ruined **Doric Temple**, a 19th-century former summer house, and then, about 100 yards (90m) further on is the modern sculpture ★★ **The Upper Room** ❾, an imaginative perspective representation of *The Last Supper* carved from 13 elm trunks by Colin Wilbourn, artist-in-residence at the cathedral from 1986–7.

Upper Room sculpture

47

In front of you now are the elegant arches of ★★ **Prebends Bridge**, built in 1778 by George Nicholson and named after the prebends, or canons, of the cathedral. It is worth crossing the pedestrianised bridge and walking a few yards north along the riverbank as far as the cottage to gain the ★★★ **classic view** of the three towers of the cathedral, rising above the woodland and red-tiled Old Fulling Mill and cascading weir in the foreground. The bridge is today perhaps most famous for the inscription at either end bearing Sir Walter Scott's much quoted description of the cathedral:

Prebends Bridge

> *Grey Towers of Durham,*
> *Yet well I love thy mixed and massive piles*
> *Half church of God, half castle 'gainst the Scot*

View from Framwellgate Bridge

Return over the bridge to visit the ★★ **Museum of Archaeology** ❿ in the Old Fulling Mill (April to October, daily 11am–4pm; November to March, Wednesday to Sunday 12.30–3pm). Run by the respected Durham University Department of Archaeology, the museum houses a permanent display of finds from Durham's history and prehistory, plus regular temporary exhibitions.

Turn left from the Museum and walk along the riverside, back under the towers and buttresses of the cathedral to the orginally 12th-century **Framwellgate Bridge** (which has a fine view of the castle and cathedral), turning right to ascend the steps to reach the cobbled and pedestrianised Silver Street and return to the Market Place.

Stepping back in time at Beamish

Route 7

Durham's Countryside

Durham – Peterlee – Seaham – Chester-le-Street – Beamish – Stanley – Lanchester – Consett – Stanhope – Bishop Auckland – Escomb – Durham (about 80 miles/128km) *See map, pages 50–1*

The very name of the county of Durham sets it apart from the rest of English counties. It is still known as *County* Durham, with its echoes of the style of Irish counties and being not quite *English* somehow.

It was the long-lasting influence of those all-powerful prince-bishops which gave Durham that extra appellation. As a virtually independent County Palatine, with control over its own parliament, laws, coinage, and army, it was entitled to the prefix – and still wears it with considerable pride.

Durham is perhaps still best known for its marvellous cathedral city, while the countryside of County Durham remains vastly underrated. It still suffers from the reputation and legacy of many years of industry, especially around the Tyne and Wear, and the county is often looked down upon for its lack of scenic beauty.

The proud heritage of that industrial legacy has not been allowed to be forgotten, however, and at the award-winning North of England Open Air Museum at Beamish – the first of its kind in the country – visitors can literally step back in time into the county's industrial past.

All aboard!

Vivid reconstructions of actual buildings, shops, cottages, pits, trams and railway stations are shown off by guides in period dress who most effectively take you back to the days of the industrial 19th century.

Now that King Coal has been firmly deposed, and that once disfiguring but culturally vital industry is virtually extinct, the valleys of Durham's interior are returning to their former greenery; and the coastal township of Seaham is a popular resort for Wearsiders.

The route starts from the county town and capital of the prince-bishops, **Durham City** (*see Route 6*). Take the A181 Hartlepool road east through pleasant countryside for nine miles to the junction with the A19 beyond Wheatley Hill and Wingate.

This dual carriageway road is then followed north around the New Town of **Peterlee**, where there is a **Tourist Information Centre** in Upper Chare (tel: 0191 586 4450). Named after Councillor Peter Lee, miner, chairman of the County Council, president of the Miners' Federation and prominent Methodist lay preacher, it was founded in 1947 to take the overspill from the Wear and Tyneside cities.

Just before you get to the town centre, pick up signs to the National Nature Reserve of ★★ **Castle Eden Dene** at Oakerside Lodge (open at all times via footpaths, Lodge open for parties if booked in advance – tel: 0191 586 0004). 'Dene' is the local name for a deep, narrow ravine running down to the sea, and Castle Eden Dene is a former 18th-century landscaped garden which has now been re-colonised by nature and turned into a 500-acre (200 hectare) nature reserve – the largest in County Durham. Twelve miles (19km) of footpaths thread the deep, heavily wooded ravine, famous for its woodland plants and ivy-covered limestone cliffs.

Castle Eden Dene

Continue on the A19 to the Seaton roundabout, where you turn right to **Seaham** – a harbour town founded by the 3rd Marquis of Londonderry in 1828 to export Durham coal to the rest of Britain. Now the coal has gone, the largely abandoned ★★ **Harbour** is used by pleasure craft and sailing boats, with a few 'cobles' used by fishermen to catch lobsters and take visitors out on sea-fishing trips. There are fine sandy beaches nearby, which are very popular on summer weekends. Lord Byron was married to Arabella Milbanke in 1815 at the **Seaham Hall Hotel**, then the family home of the Milbankes.

The adjacent clifftop Saxon/Norman ★★ **Church of St Mary** is reached along a track and stands in romantic isolation surrounded by a belt of stunted trees. It has Roman stones built into its walls and the mysterious design of a priest's hand incised into a niche in the chancel.

Seaham harbour

Back on the Seaton roundabout, take the A19 north, turning west at the third exit onto the B-road which leads to **Houghton-le-Spring** (pronounced 'Hoton'). This former

Priest's hand in St Mary's Church

St Mary and St Cuthbert

market and later mining town is savagely dissected by the A690 Durham-Sunderland road, but it has a fine Norman **Parish Church**, with memorials to Bernard Gilpin (1517–83), 'the Apostle of the North', and Sir Francis Blake, the noted 18th-century mathematician. Near the church is the **Kepier Grammar School**, founded by Gilpin, and, across the A690, the great square three-storeyed Elizabethan **Old Hall**.

From Houghton, follow the A182 across the A1(M) to reach **Chester-le-Street**, a busy market town astride a former Roman road, which is watched over by the elegant 14th-century spire of the mainly Early English ★★ **Parish Church of St Mary and St Cuthbert**, one of the resting places of the body of St Cuthbert on its peripatetic progress to Durham. The original church was Saxon, and there are some Saxon stones in the south wall. Don't miss the long line of Lumley effigies in the north aisle, or the ★★ **Anchorite's Cell** (or Anker House or Anchorage), where a hermit monk was in residence until the Dissolution of the Monasteries, and which is now a fascinating museum.

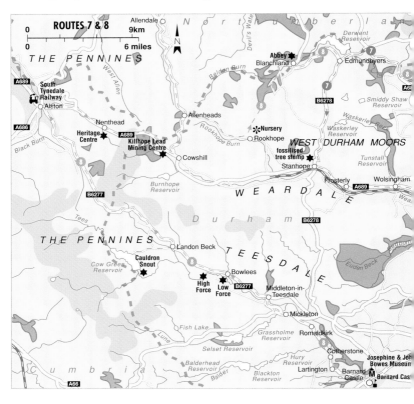

Nearby, set in well-wooded grounds, is **Lumley Castle** (now a private hotel), seat of the Lumley family for 600 years and extensively re-fashioned by Vanbrugh for the 2nd Earl of Scarborough. Visitors can now enjoy medieval banquets in this perfect setting.

Leaving Chester-le-Street by the A693 heading west towards Stanley, after about 4 miles (6.5km) you pass the entrance on the right to the ★★★ **North of England Open Air Museum** at **Beamish** (mid-April to late October, daily 10am–5pm, last admission 3pm (6pm in school summer holiday, last admission 4pm); late October to early April, town only 10am–4pm, last admission 3pm, closed Monday and Friday).

Created in 1970, this pioneering open-air museum is one of the leading tourist attractions in the North East, vividly recreating the industrial and social past of the region by means of carefully reconstructed buildings and attendants in period dress. All the buildings have been taken from sites in the area and reconstructed. They range from the ★★★ **Victorian town**, complete with cobbled streets,

Victorian shop at Beamish

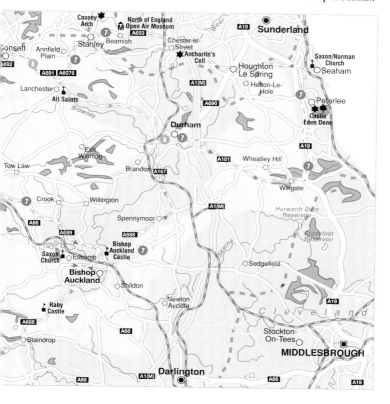

Inside a pit cottage

Cleaning out the stables

shops, pub, stables, park and ornamental bandstand, to a railway station (taken from Rowley, a small village near Consett), where steam trains including a replica of George Stephenson's 'Locomotion' can be seen.

★★ **Home Farm** stands where it always has, and includes local breeds of livestock with a programme of breeding for some of the rarer animals, and a restored farmhouse. The ★★★ **Colliery** occupies an important area of the museum site, as might be expected in view of the importance of the coal industry to the area in the past. The tall stone engine house contains a steam winder built in 1855 for the Beamish Colliery, and nearby is the ★★ **Drift Mine** and ★★ **Pit Cottages** where the miners of Hetton-le-Hole originally lived.

The museum, winner of both European and British Museum of the Year awards, is constantly being expanded and exhibits added, and at least two to four hours should be allowed to obtain full benefit from a visit.

From **Beamish**, continue west on the A693. A worthwhile diversion 2 miles (3.5km) to the north of **Stanley** off the B6076 Newcastle road is ★ **The Causey Arch** (open at all times), which is claimed to be the oldest railway bridge in the world. The single-span structure was built in 1725–6 by Ralph Wood, orginally to carry horse-drawn coal waggons 80ft (24m) above a deep ravine. It is now the centrepiece of a pleasant picnic area served by the Tanfield Steam Railway, which runs between Sunniside and East Tanfield. From the car park, there are good footpaths leading to the top of the arch and through the ravine.

After bypassing Stanley, take another diversion south on the A6076 to the village of **Lanchester**, which owes its existence to the Romans, who built their fort of *Longovicium* here on their highway of Dere Street. ★★ **All Saints Parish Church** is one of County Durham's largest and finest parish churches, and it is generally thought that the massive quoins and monolithic columns of the nave came from the Roman fort. The church is Norman and Early English, and was formerly collegiate, with a staff of prebendaries which also served the Bishop of Durham.

From Lanchester, the A691 joins the A692 near the former steel-making town of **Consett**, where some of the gaunt remains of this industry still haunt the skyline. From **Consett** head west on the B6278 towards **Stanhope**, crossing the A68 and into the Durham moors, going past the **Derwent Reservoir** (*see Route 8, page 59*) and the pretty village of **Edmundbyers**, where the **parish church** has interior woodwork from churches all over the country.

The road now climbs steeply to the south, over the wild and desolate West Durham Moors between Bolt's Law (1,773ft/540m) to the right and radio mast-topped Collier

Over the West Durham Moors

Law (1,694ft/516m) to the left. A gradual descent across Stanhope Common leads down into ★ **Stanhope**. Founded on the wealth from the rich lead mines of the dale, Stanhope is often called 'the Capital of Weardale'. The broad main street leads to the square and the ★ **Parish Church of St Thomas**, which is mainly 12th and 14th century, but has a Saxon font and a Roman altar found on the moors. In the churchyard is the fossilised stump of a 250 million-year-old tree. **Stanhope Castle** (private), built in 1798 for Cuthbert Rippon, MP for Gateshead, faces the square.

Stanhope's parish church

From **Stanhope**, the route follows the A689 for 17 miles (27km) down the wooded valley of the River Wear, through **Frosterley** and **Wolsingham** to **Crook** and eventually to **Bishop Auckland**.

There is a strangly Continental air to the Market Square of Bishop Auckland, with the tall, pinnacled **Town Hall** and **Parish Church** (1847), and imposing, clock-capped gateway to ★★ **Bishop Auckland Castle** (May, June and September, Friday and Sunday 2–5pm; July, Thursday, Friday and Sunday 2–5pm; August, Thursday to Sunday 2–5pm; last admission 30 minutes before closing). The castle has been the country residence of the bishops of Durham since Norman times, and is now the official residence of the present Bishop. The rooms open to the public include the **Chapel**, said to be the largest private chapel in Europe, the **State Rooms**, including the **Bishop's Throne Room**, and the medieval **Kitchens**, which currently house an exhibition on the life of St Cuthbert and the history of the Durham Diocese. The adjacent ★ **Bishop's Park** (daily 7am to sunset) has an 18th-century mock-Gothic deercote, or shelter, in its grounds.

53

Before leaving Bishop Auckland, it is worth retracing your steps slightly to take the B6282 towards **Etherley** for about a mile from the town centre, where a minor road leads off over the railway line and through a council estate to the right, to **Escomb**. Here, the ★★★ **Parish Church of St John the Evangelist** (summer, daily 9am–6pm; winter, 9am–4pm; obtain the key from No. 22, Saxon Green, Escomb – opposite the church) has been described as 'after Durham Cathedral, the most impressive ecclesiastical building in the county'. It is one of those worldwide rarities – a virtually complete Saxon church, dating from around AD680 (so it has echoes of Cuthbert and Bede). Its tall nave, beamed roof and narrow windows are a marvellous survival, made all the more poignant for the church's unlikely setting. Some of the stones of Escomb church are known to have come from the Roman fort at nearby Binchester, across the River Wear.

Escomb's Saxon jewel

From Bishop Auckland, it is 11 miles (17km) back to Durham along the A688 and A167.

Typical of Teesdale: whitewashed barns

Route 8

North Pennines

Durham – Raby Castle – Barnard Castle – Middleton-in-Teesdale – High Force – Alston – Killhope Lead Mining Centre – Allendale – Blanchland – Durham (about 100 miles/160kms) *See map, pages 50–1*

The Killhope Wheel

The North Pennines have been dubbed 'England's Last Wilderness' by the slogan-conscious tourist board, but in reality they are just like anywhere else in Britain, where wilderness is a purely relative term.

Even the wildest parts of the high, peat and heather-covered moorland plateau of the North Pennines Area of Outstanding Natural Beauty (AONB) has largely been created by Man's activity, through centuries of sheep grazing and the management of the moors for the shooting of red grouse. The many whitewashed farmhouses in the area are reminders of the all-pervading influence of the Raby Castle estate, from its medieval stronghold near Staindrop.

And the dales of the North Pennines were once one of the most important centres in the world for the mining of lead. Evidence of 'th' owd man', as the lead miners are known, is still to be found in many places, and the Killhope Lead Mining Centre in Upper Weardale graphically tells the story of their industry.

The North Pennines, covering 765 square miles (1,983 sq. km) is the largest AONB in the country, designated in 1978 to protect its natural scenic beauty as well as its industrial past. Geologically, the region is typically Pennine – the bedrocks are from the Carboniferous period, in the familiar series of limestone, gritstone and shales – all slightly tilted towards the east where the river valleys of the Tyne, Tees, Wear and Derwent run down towards their eventual destination in the North Sea. The scenic highlights of the region are found, however, where fault lines have allowed the intrusion of the hard, igneous Whin Sill (which we have already met on Hadrian's Wall and the Northumberland coast) through these sedimentary rocks to create some of the finest landforms in the north of England. They include the spectacular waterfalls of High Force – England's biggest – and Cauldron Snout, both of which can be visited from this route.

Raby Castle

The route starts from the historic cathedral city of **Durham** (*see Route 6*), taking the A167 Darlington road south for 5 miles (8km) to its junction with the A688, where it turns right through **Spennymoor** and **Bishop Auckland** (*see Route 7, page 53*). After passing through **West Auckland**, the route continues southwest and after about 6 miles (10km), signs on the right indicate the walled entrance to ★★★ **Raby Castle and Gardens** (Easter, Saturday to Wednesday but closed for the rest of April; May and June, Wednesday and Sunday only; July to September, daily except Saturday; also open Bank Holiday weekends, Saturday to Wednesday. Castle open 1–5pm, gardens 11am–5.30pm).

Raby Castle, set in its 200-acre (80-hectare) deer park, has been the home of Lord Barnard's family for over 350 years, and it is one of the country's most impressive and complete medieval castles. According to legend, it was King Canute (1017–36) who built the first castle here, but the bulk of the magnificent building seen today dates from the 14th century and was the work of Lord Ralph Neville of Raby, hero of the Battle of Neville's Cross in 1346. Particularly impressive are **Clifford's Tower** and the 600-year-old **Kitchen**, with its 14th-century vaulted roof and louvre, stone-flagged floors and great fireplaces. The **State Rooms** are magnificent in their opulence and mainly the work of William Burn, who also built the dominating **Octagon Tower** in the 1840s. The Palladian-faced **Stables** are the work of John Carr and contain a remarkable collection of horse-drawn coaches and carriages, while the walled **Gardens**, bounded by a ha-ha (dry ditch) provide a perfect setting to admire the **Park** with its lake and herds of fallow deer.

Carriage in the stables

The castle gardens

Back on the A688, the route passes through the old market town of **Staindrop**, where the mainly 13th-century ★★ **Parish Church of St Mary** is in a pretty setting near the green and has a Saxon nave and many Norman remains. As might be expected for an estate settlement such as this, there are impressive memorial tombs in oak, alabaster and marble, to the Nevilles of nearby Raby.

The Butter Market in 'Barney'

The castle's Balliol Tower

Arriving in style at the Bowes Museum

It is 6 miles (10km) now to ★★ **Barnard Castle**, or 'Barney' as the capital town of Teesdale is locally known. On Wednesday – market day – the town is crowded with farmers from the length of the Upper Tees, who bring in their stock to be sold and to shop at the stalls which fill the **Butter Market**, with its eight-sided bell tower where butter was once kept to keep cool, **Thorngate** and **Newgate**. There are many interesting buildings in the town, most dating from the 18th century, the oldest being ★★ **Blagroves House** (now a restaurant), a delightful, leaning 16th-century house in **The Bank** with three-storey high gabled bay windows, where allegedly Oliver Cromwell was once entertained.

But the most impressive building in Barnard Castle is, of course, its eponymous ★★★ **Castle** (English Heritage; 27 March to 30 September, daily 10am–6pm; October, 10am–4pm; November to March, 10am–4pm, closed on Monday and Tuesday and at Christmas). Standing proudly on their clifftop site above the Tees, these towering ruins date from Bernard Balliol's (who gave the town its other name) first building of 1125. Highlights are the 13th-century **Northam Tower**, the **Round** (or Balliol) **Tower**, and the remains of the 15th-century **Great Chamber**, with its oriel window, and the **Great Hall**. The best view of the castle is from the river near the graceful bridge over the Tees, dating from 1569.

Follow **Newgate** out of **Barnard Castle**, and within half a mile you come to one of the most extraordinary museums and country houses in Britain, the ★★★ **Josephine and John Bowes Museum** (Monday to Saturday 10am–5.30pm, Sunday 2–5pm; closes at 5pm in March, April and October, and 4pm November to February). Looking more like a grand French château than a regional museum on the outskirts of an English country town, the Bowes Museum was designed by the French architect, Jules Pellechet, for John Bowes, the illegitimate son of the 10th Earl of Strathmore, from whom he had inherited his vast County Durham estates. (He married a French actress, Josephine Benoite, Countess of Montalbo, hence the museum's name).

Bowes died before the museum opened in 1892, but his legacy filled the incredible house with one of the finest collections of French and Spanish paintings in the country. Other rooms in this sumptuous house are devoted to collections of Continental and English furniture and china, reconstructions of rooms from other English houses, and local antiquities from southwest Durham, ranging from prehistoric and Roman times to the 19th century.

Take the B6277 from **Barnard Castle** to follow the southern bank of the Tees into the heart of beautiful **Teesdale**,

Low Force waterfall

passing through **Lartington** to ★★**Cotherstone**, which is many people's favourite Teesdale village. Famous for its soft cheese (still made locally), Cotherstone stands high above the junction of the Tees with the Balder with charming, green-fronted cottages lining the winding main street.

The next village is **Romaldkirk**, which rivals **Cotherstone** for its pretty greens. It takes its name from the unusual dedication of its spacious, mainly 14th-century Decorated-style ★★**Parish Church** on the lower green, which is sometimes known as the 'Cathedral of the Dale'.

57

Seven miles (11km) from Barnard Castle is **Mickleton**, after which the road turns sharply right to cross the river and enter ★★**Middleton-in-Teesdale**, the major township of Upper Teesdale and a staging post on the Pennine Way. Here the moors start to crowd in on the river, and this charming little town, full of interesting, mainly 19th-century buildings and winding alleyways, is a superb centre for their exploration. Although originally a Saxon settlement, Middleton's wealth was founded on lead mining, and it was formerly the headquarters of the London Lead Company, which had its offices at Middleton House (private) on the hill to the northwest. The **Bainbridge Memorial Fountain** (1877) in the centre of town, with its Victorian Gothic cast-iron canopy, commemorates a former manager.

Middleton's memorial fountain and the Wynch Bridge at Bowlees

Two miles (3.5km) further up the B6277 at **Bowlees**, a path across the field opposite the telephone box leads to the pedestrian ★**Wynch Bridge**, said to be the earliest suspension bridge in Europe. It was built for the use of lead miners in 1744 but rebuilt in 1828 after it collapsed. Just a few yards upstream from here along the Pennine Way is ★★**Low Force**, the smaller but prettier sister waterfall of the more famous High Force. (Force comes from the Old Norse *foss*, meaning waterfall.) Also at **Bowlees**, housed in the former Methodist Chapel, is the ★**Bowlees**

High Force from the top

Hikers at Cow Green

Alston: South Tyndale Railway

Visitor Centre (1 April to 30 September, daily 10.30am–5pm; 1 October to 31 March, Saturday and Sunday 11am–4pm). There are displays on wildlife and history.

Back on the road, the next landmark is the **High Force Hotel** on the right, which has a large car park and public toilets. This enables the visitor, for a small charge, to cross the road and take the path through the riverside trees to visit England's greatest waterfall, the magnificent ★★★ **High Force**. When the Tees is in spate, this is one of the most elemental places in the Pennines available to the normal pedestrian. The peat-stained waters crash 70ft (21m) over a glistening black lip of Whin Sill into a dark, tree-fringed plunge pool, sending up plumes of spray.

The route now continues northwest to reach the tiny moorland hamlet of **Langdon Beck**, where a sign leads left onto a cattle-gridded minor road towards ★★ **Cow Green Reservoir and Nature Trail**. The construction of the reservoir in 1970 was the cause of major controversy because rare Ice Age relict flora were destroyed in the process. The nature trail leads from the reservoir car park for about a mile to the great concrete **Cow Green Dam** and a short but demanding scramble down an outcrop of Whin Sill to the spectacular but now artificially-controlled 200-ft (61m) waterfall of ★★ **Cauldron Snout**, another landmark on the **Pennine Way**.

Back on the B6277, the road now climbs for another 5 moorland miles (8km) to reach its high point at 1,958ft (597m), before crossing the watershed below Burnhope Seat (2,448/746m) and descending to **Alston**, across the Cumbrian border in the valley of the River South Tyne.

Alston is an ideal centre for exploring the North Pennines, and has a wealth of accommodation and refreshment opportunities. The **Tourist Information Centre** is at the beautifully-restored Railway Station from where the narrow-guage **South Tynedale Railway** runs regular steam and diesel-hauled passenger trips beside the river. (28 March to 6 April, daily 11am–4pm; 7 April to 30 May, Saturday, Sunday and Bank Holidays 11am–4pm; June and September, Thursday, Saturday and Sunday 11am–4pm; 1 July to 31 August, daily 11am–4pm; October, Saturday and Sunday, noon–5pm.)

From **Alston**, take the A689 Bishop Auckland road which climbs to ★★ **Nenthead**, a planned village and 'company town' of the London Lead Company. The socially innovative Quaker-run company provided a **Reading Room** (the first free library in England), and in what is now the **Village Hall**, the earliest compulsory schooling in the country for its employees and their families. Their story is told in the ★★ **Nenthead Heritage Centre** (28 March to 31 October, daily 10.30am–5pm).

After crossing the watershed into County Durham, the road descends into Weardale, and 2 miles (3.5km) before the hamlet of Cowshill, on the right, is the ★★★ **Killhope Lead Mining Centre** (April to October, daily 10.30am–5pm; Sunday only in November, 10.30am–4pm; last admission 30 minutes before closing). This exciting interpretive centre explores the life of the North Pennine lead miner, and the recently opened Park Level Mine – the most extensive show mine in the north of England – enables the visitor, suitably equipped, to go underground in the footsteps of the miners. But the most impressive artefact for many visitors is the **Killhope Wheel**, the enormous, 33½-ft (10m) diameter iron water wheel which was used to crush the lead ore (*galena*) brought up from the levels which scar the hillsides all around. Having been crushed, the ore was washed, and school parties and the general public can now get involved in this activity.

Washing ore at Killhope

The B6295 leads north from **Cowshill** to **Allenheads**, another lead mining village high in the hills, and said to be the highest village in England. From here, it is worth continuing the descent northwards for 8 miles (13km) to ★ **Allendale Town**, whose attractive square is famous as the venue for the Allendale Fire Festival (*see Culture, page 64*). Less well known about the town is the fact that at midday GMT, the latitude and longditude readings of the **sundial** on the wall of the church are said to substantiate its claim to being the geographical centre of Britain.

Allendale's sundial **59**

Back at Allenheads, take the minor road towards **Rookhope**, where at 1,100ft (335m) there is one of the highest nurseries in Britain, perhaps not surprisingly specialising in hardy northern varieties!

Just before entering Rookhope, another lonely moorland road leads north to descend into the Derwent Valley to the neat, monastic village of ★★ **Blanchland**, one of Northumbria's most picturesque villages whose mellow stone buildings are based around the ground plan of an 800-year-old former **Abbey**, founded in 1169 by a group of a dozen monks from the Premonstratensian order (an off-shoot of the white-robed Cistercians). The **Gatehouse** now serves as the village post office, and the **Abbot's Lodge** is now the Lord Crewe Arms. The squat tower of the ★ **Parish Church of St Mary** dominates the village and is the largest remaining part of the **Abbey Church**, which was rebuilt in the 18th century by Lord Crewe after its destruction during the Dissolution.

Blanchland

The B6306 leads down to the shores of the **Derwent Reservoir** and past the **Pow Hill Country Park** to the village of **Edmundbyers** (*see Route 7, page 52*). Here the route turns left to join the A68, then bypasses **Consett** on the A692 before following the A691 back to **Durham**.

The Historic Landscape

Opposite:
Dunstanburgh Castle

The historic palimpsest of hillforts, settlements and cup-and-ring stones seen so graphically in the Lordenshaws area near Rothbury (*see Route 3, page 31*) is by no means unique in Northumbria.

The imprint of these multi-layered facets of human history is still plainly visible in many places in the rough grasslands of the Cheviots. An example is the great twin-summited Iron Age hillfort and massive embankments of the Yeavering Bell on the northern edge of the hills, which dominate the valley of the River Glen, and the incongruous roadside monument which marks the site of the Saxon King Edwin's palace of *Ad Gefrin* (*see Route 1, page 21*). South of here, the landscape is covered with ancient sites, and near Hindhope, the ring ditches of the Woden Law hillfort are among half a dozen overlooking the upper reaches of the Kale Water and Capehope Burns. The Iron Age was obviously a period of settlement in well-organised communities in the highlands of the Simonside Fells and Cheviots.

Cup and ring stone at Lordenshaws

But the footprint of the next invaders, the Romans, is also still fresh in these hills. The great Roman northern highway of Dere Street, which linked Lanchester with Carlisle, runs just below Woden Law and descends to the still visible earthworks of the twin Roman marching camps at Pennymuir in the plain below. To the south, Dere Street follows the modern line of the Pennine Way to perhaps the best preserved of the Cheviot Roman camps at Chew Green (*Ad Fines*), near the source of the Coquet below the Roman Signal Station on Brownhart Law.

St Aidan

But, of course, the most famous reminder of Roman might in Northumbria is Hadrian's Wall, a World Heritage Site and one of the best preserved examples of Roman military architecture in the whole of Europe, built over a length of 73 miles (117km) to protect the northern limits of the empire from marauding tribes of Scots. Details of the Wall's construction and significance are explained elsewhere in this book (*see pages 7–8*), and its main attractions are visited in Route 5 (*see page 37*).

The history books tell us that after the Roman legions left to defend their homeland, Northumbria, like the rest of Britain, was plunged into the cultural blackout of the so-called Dark Ages. But if there is one region of Britain which disproves that traditional theory, it is here.

The richness of the Celtic art and sculpture from Northumbria proves beyond any doubt that, far from being a cultural vacuum, the Dark Ages saw a tremendous flowering of artistry and culture – and the first dawning of Christianity in England (*see page 63*). The Bewcastle Cross, just across the Cumbrian border on the edge of

61

the Border Forest Park, is a wonderful example of the vigorous sculpture of the age, while the font of Rothbury church is made from another carved Saxon cross shaft.

The remote kingdom of Northumbria turned out to be a thorn in the side of William the Conqueror, after his invasion of Britain in 1066. Three years after Hastings, he had to put down a Danish-inspired rebellion, and built the first castle at Durham in 1072.

The Norman Chapel in Durham Castle

With a foothold established in Durham, the Normans embarked on the infamous 'Harrying of the North' in 1080, when Bishop Odo of Bayeaux laid waste 'every field and dwelling between York and Durham'. They followed this by building more castles, including the classic motte and bailey construction in Elsdon; the original stone keep and battlements on the site of the Saxon King Ida's settlement at Bamburgh; Bernard Balliol's commanding keep and castle overlooking the Tees at Barnard Castle; and dramatic Dunstanburgh near Craster. Baronial castles sprung up along the Northumbrian coast, such as Alnwick and Warkworth, as the Norman overlords tried to keep the troublesome locals under their Feudal control.

Eventually, matters settled down and local people returned to the traditional pastoral farming of the hills. Markets sprung up in towns like Hexham, Rothbury and Barnard Castle, but the Border spirit of lawlessness was never far below the surface, and it still regularly broke loose when the reivers, or 'steel bonnets', took to the hills (*see pages 8–9*).

More formal battles took place between the English and the Scots: at Otterburn in 1388, when Scots, under the leadership of James, Earl of Douglas, defeated the English, under Harry 'Hotspur' Percy, son of the 1st Earl of Northumberland; and at Flodden Field, when the English turned the tables in 1513.

The Union of the English and Scottish crowns in 1603 signalled the end of the worst of the cross-Border conflicts, and then, after the scare of the Jacobite Rebellion, the first waves of the Industrial Revolution spread out into the hills of the North Pennines. Lead deposits in the South Tyne and Teesdale began to be exploited by companies like the Quaker-inspired London Lead Company, based at Middleton-in-Teesdale. Unlike many of their industrialist counterparts in the fast-expanding cities of Newcastle and Middlesbrough, these Quaker benefactors were considerate to their employees, as their 'model village' of Nenthead shows (*see Route 8, page 58*).

Mine waggons at Killhope

Visitors can experience these Pennine lead mines at the Killhope Lead Mining Centre in Weardale (*see Route 8, page 59*), and taste what life was like in a Victorian town of the north east at the award-winning Beamish Open Air Museum, near Stanley (*see Route 7, page 51*).

62

St Cuthbert – The Fire of the North

Cuthbert, the greatest of the northern saints, was born in the Scottish Borders in 635. It was while tending his sheep in the Lammermuir Hills that he saw a vision of a great light and angels in the sky, and took it as a sign to enter the monastery of Melrose, vowing to spread the Christian message throughout Northumbria.

In the same year as Cuthbert's birth, the Northumbrian King Oswald won a famous victory over Welsh and Mercian invaders near Hexham. He sent for St Aidan from Iona to spread the Christian message throughout his now-settled kingdom. Soon after, Aidan and 12 companions founded the first monastery at Lindisfarne. This tiny rocky island, cut off by the tides from the mainland twice each day, was to become the cradle of Christianity in the north-east, and later for the rest of Europe. Aidan was succeeded by St Cuthbert in 664.

*St Cuthbert Window
in Durham Cathedral*

Christianity had been introduced to Northumbria by Paulinus, who organised a mass baptism at King Edwin's palace of *Ad Gefrin* in 627. But it was Cuthbert – 'the Fire of the North' – who really ignited the Christian flame in the region. The fame of his gift for healing spread far and wide and he was frequently called to other monasteries and to preach and heal throughout the north. But Cuthbert preferred solitude, and he often withdrew to live the life of a hermit in a tiny cell on the rocky island of Inner Farne.

63

There are many legends associated with St Cuthbert, mostly related by the Venerable Bede, who wrote the first *Ecclesiastical History of the English People* from his cell at Jarrow. Among these is the tale of the sea otters drying Cuthbert's feet and warming him with their breath after he had spent a night praying in the cold North Sea. His love for animals was characteristic, and the eider ducks still found around the Farne Islands are known as St Cuthbert's (or Cuddy's) ducks, because he had tamed them.

Lindisfarne Gospels

After his death in 687, Cuthbert was buried on Lindisfarne, and it was shortly after this that an unknown monk began work on the famous Lindisfarne Gospels, perhaps the most wonderful artistic and cultural legacy left by these pioneering Christians. The beautifully illuminated manuscripts are now in the British Museum in London.

Cuthbert's body was not destined to stay on his beloved Lindisfarne, or Holy Island. After a series of Viking raids on the coast, monks removed it, first to Chester-le-Street and later to Ripon, before it eventually ended up, in 995, on the peninsula in the River Wear known as Dunholme – modern Durham. Today, the remains of the famous Celtic saint reside in the Lady Chapel behind the altar of the great Norman cathedral, while those of his great chronicler, Bede, are at the opposite end in the Galilee Chapel.

The Allendale Fire Festival

Folklore and Festivals

At 30 minutes to midnight on New Year's Eve, a great crowd of people starts to assemble in the market square of Allendale Town, the small (pop. 600) township at the head of the East and West Allen Rivers in County Durham.

What happens next is unique in England and only found elsewhere at the *Up Helly Aa* ceremony in Shetland, where a Viking longboat is ritually burned. They are gathering for the **Allendale Fire Festival** or *Tar Barling* ceremony – a midwinter festival of unknown origins, but which must date back at least to Celtic times.

As the sun reaches its lowest point of the year, the ceremony marks the death of the old year and the rebirth and promise of the new. Some experts believe that it is linked symbolically to the rebirth of the Norse god of vegetation, Balder, and the Bel, or *Baal*, festivals held elsewhere in northern Europe.

The bonfire lights up the square

Whatever the origins, the Allendale Festival begins as a group of about 40 local men known as 'guisers' appear, each carrying a cut-off blazing barrel of fire on his head. The column of men, led by one carrying a torch, parades around the market square and finally approaches the huge bonfire of wood and more petrol-filled barrels which is placed in its centre. Then, at the stroke of midnight, the guisers tip their blazing loads one by one onto the central bonfire, which ignites in a huge fireball that lights up the square and the whole town.

The Allendale New Year's Eve Fire Festival is matched on a smaller scale by a similar midsummer ceremony known as the **Whalton Baal Fire**, when a large bonfire is lit on the village green in this small village near Morpeth on 4 July every year. These pagan festivals echo the region's distant past and worship of what is sometimes known as 'the Old Religion', which is still sometimes kept alive in the remote hills and dales of Northumbria.

Another way in which the ancient culture of the region is continued is through the Northumbrian dialect which, in truth, is more of a separate language when heard in full flow. Although to the uninitiated it may mistakenly and loosely be categorised as 'Geordie', in fact the true Northumbrian tongue derives directly from the Anglo-Northumbrian speech which would be recognised by King Ida of Bamburgh, St Cuthbert, Bede, Harry Hotspur of Otterburn and Shakespeare's *King Henry V*. Words like 'listy' (energetic); 'hinny' (a term of endearment) and 'lippen' (trust) all have a lineage which speaks from that ancient past.

The finest expression of that lilting, musical Northumbrian tongue is through the **songs and ballads** which are passed on from father to son, mother to daughter, and which can still be heard sung in local hostelries. The most famous of these are the Border Ballads, first collected and probably saved for posterity by Sir Walter Scott in his *Minstrelsy of the Scottish Border*. When accompanied by the Northumbrian small-pipes – a smaller and sweeter sounding local version of the Scottish bag-pipes – these wistful, simple but highly evocative ballads tell much of the region's troubled past. The Northumbrian pipes are inflated not by a mouth-piece but by bellows held under the arm, and can be seen and heard in the Morpeth Chantry Bagpipe Museum in Bridge Street, Morpeth.

Northumbrian small-pipes in Morpeth

The great social gathering where all these folk traditions are brought together is the **Morpeth Northumbrian Gathering**, usually held in April on the weekend following Easter. This is a wonderful festival of traditional music, song and dance, at which there are competitions for clog-dancing, Northumbrian small-pipe playing and ballad singing.

Among the other festivals of the region is the Alnwick **Shrove Tuesday Football Game**, when two huge teams representing two parishes fight it out in the castle park and over, and often in, the River Aln in a predecessor of the modern game, most famously practised locally by Newcastle United's 'Toon (town) Army'. Alnwick also has its **Fair** at the end of June each year (*see page 17*), and in the first week of August holds its **International Music Festival**, when the market place becomes the focal point of music and dance performed by groups and troupes from all over the world. The ceremony of **Riding the Bounds** still takes place on May Day at Berwick-upon-Tweed, just across the Scottish Border, when the boundaries of the ancient border borough are marked; and the walls of the town, improved by Mary Tudor in 1555, are ritually run around in early September.

International Music Festival in Alnwick

Food and Drink

For a true taste of Northumbria, the visitor should try some of the local delicacies for which the region is justly famous. Apart from the universally acclaimed Newcastle Brown Ale, chief among these are the seafoods from the North Sea coast.

Craster kippers, naturally and traditionally oak-smoked in this tiny fishing village near Alnwick, give an unforgettable taste, far removed from the frozen supermarket variety. Shellfish, like lobsters and crabs, are freshly caught from the fishing port of North Shields and exported all over Europe. A visit to the North Shields Fish Quay Festival in May is highly recommended.

Local cheeses include Cotherstone, a mild full-fat cheese rather like Wensleydale but softer and with its own distinctive flavour. It was once produced by farmers' wives in every farmstead in Teesdale, but is now only made on one farm in the pretty village of Cotherstone high above the Tees, and is on sale in Barnard Castle and other local outlets. There is also a smoked version. Redesdale cheese was also formerly widely produced in the valley of that name, and although it can still be found for sale around the village of Otterburn, it is something of a rarity today.

Cotherstone cheese

67

Other local delicacies often reflect poorer times when meat was not so freely available. They include the famous Northumbrian stotty cakes, fromenty (boiled barley, milk and sugar), and plum-broth (meat, fruit and spices minced together). On Carlin Sunday, some local pubs still provide saucers of hard, fried grey peas of the local Carlin variety, and at Christmas 'Yule Babbies' are still cooked – the baby being made from pastry and currants.

Restaurant selection

The following cafés and restaurants are just a small selection from some of Northumbria's most popular. They are listed according to the following broad categories: £££ = expensive; ££ = moderate; £ = inexpensive.

Alnwick
Bark Pot Tearoom, Craster, Alnwick, tel: 01665 576286. Family-run tearoom in an attractive new building on the edge of this popular coastal village. Equipped with a large terrace, it caters to the lunchtime pangs of walkers and other trippers with traditional home baking. £

Amble
Charlies Restaurant, Albert Street, Amble, tel: 01665 710206. This is one of the finest fish and chip restaurants in Northumbria. It also provides takeaway trade and has an extensive subsidiary menu. £.

Charlies Restaurant

Bamburgh

Copper Kettle Tearooms, Front Street, Bamburgh, tel:
01668 214315. Atmospheric café in 18th-century house
featuring oak-beamed ceiling and unique carved panelling.
Local favourites include the gingerbread and the cherry
madeira, but light lunches are also served and there is a
garden patio. Wide selection of teas and coffees. £.

Barnard Castle

Rose and Crown Hotel, Romaldkirk, Barnard Castle, tel:
01833 650213. Just outside the town in one of Teesdale's
prettiest villages, the award-winning Rose and Crown is
recommended in all the leading food guides. Specialises
in first-class, English cooking. ££.

Bellingham

Riverdale Hall Hotel & Restaurant, Bellingham, tel:
01434 220254. The first hotel in Northumberland to win
the RAC Merit Award for its food and hospitality. Table
booking is advisable at this popular venue. £££.

68

Popinjay's

Berwick-upon-Tweed

Popinjay's Restaurant, Hide Hill, Berwick, tel: 01289
307237. A modest café/restaurant which provides good,
wholesome, home-cooked food. £.

Blanchland

Lord Crewe Arms

Lord Crewe Arms, Blanchland, tel: 01434 675251. In the
former lodgings of the Abbot of Blanchland Abbey, the
Lord Crewe Arms boasts an award-winning restaurant under the direction of chef Ian Press. £££.

Hexham

Langley Castle Hotel, Langley-on-Tyne, Hexham, tel:
01434 68888. The intimate Josephine Restaurant provides
fine foods in the splendid surroundings of this 14th-cen-
tury fortified castle. Booking essential. £££.

Otterburn

The Border Reiver, Otterburn, tel: 01830 520682. This
award-winning café on the A696 prides itself on its home
cooking. As well as its famous all-day breakfasts, it claims
to have 'the best burgers in the borders'. The A1 steak
sandwich is another speciality, but vegetarians are catered
for as well. £

Wooler

Tankerville Arms, Cottage Road, Wooler, tel: 01668
281387. This 17th-century former coaching inn provides
fine food and excellent service. It is highly commended
by the tourist board. ££.

Active Holidays

Northumberland has been called the country's 'Empty Quarter', and if you want to get away from it all and escape from the crowds, there are few better places in England. The Northumberland National Park, which covers 405 square miles (1,049 sq. km) between Hadrian's Wall and the Cheviots, receives only about a million visitors a year, making it by far the least-visited of any in Britain. And despite the best efforts of the Tourist Board, which advertises the North Pennines as 'England's Last Wilderness', they too manage to retain that feeling of uncrowded remoteness.

Walking

Walking is the best way to see and appreciate the variety of scenery and countryside in the region. The final 130 miles (210km) of the **Pennine Way** run through the area, from Middleton-in-Teesdale to the Cheviots. But this stretch, especially the route over the Cheviots, is generally accepted as being one of the toughest of this classic backpacker's marathon. After heading up the Tees past High Force and Cauldron Snout, the route crosses into Cumbria to take in its high point of Cross Fell. Then from Alston and Greenhead it turns east again to meet Hadrian's Wall and then north through the conifers of the Border Forest to Bellingham. Over Coquet Head, the route takes to the Border Ridge of the Cheviots, over Windy Gyle, Cairn Hill, Auchope Cairn and The Schil, to descend finally to journey's end at the Border Hotel, Kirk Yetholm.

If you intend to tackle the Cheviots, you will need to be properly equipped with good boots and wind and waterproof clothing, plus a map and compass. The weather here can change quickly, and the going is extremely arduous, often over soft and sticky peat bogs.

Walking the Wall near Crag Lough

69

Pennine Way at Thirlwall Castle

Wayfarers at Middleton

The only problem of access to these northern hills is the presence of the Otterburn Military Training Area, north of the village from which it takes its name. Covering 58,000 acres (23,466 hectares), this NATO training base is scheduled for a major redevelopment, and access is severely restricted when live firing is taking place. Red flags or lamps are displayed and barriers closed at these times. Otherwise, walkers are advised not to touch or pick up any objects lying on the ground, as they could explode.

Warning flag near Otterburn

70

But there is plenty of much easier, and safer, walking to be had in the region, and the Northumberland National Park's excellent walking guides, *Walks in Reiver Country* and *Walks in High Hills Country*, are highly recommended. The walks described range between 2 and 14 miles (3–22km), and there is a wealth of interesting extra information imparted on each.

For a taster, try the short, 3-mile (5km) stroll from Bellingham up and over the Hareshaw Burn via six footbridges and through the flower-rich Blakelaw and Linn Plantations to **Hareshaw Linn**, a graceful little waterfall in its own mini-gorge, now owned and sensitively managed by the National Park Authority.

For a more strenuous introduction to the hills, the 5½-mile (9km) walk from Monthooly in the **College Valley** of the Cheviots to The Schil (permit from Sale and Partners, Glendale Road, Wooler) is recommended, as are any of the numerous trails in the glorious Harthope Valley (for details, *see Route 1, page 21*). More distant views of the Cheviots can be enjoyed while hiking the 8-mile (13km) **Simonside Ridge** near Rothbury (*see Route 3*).

A number of car parks and the regular **Hadrian's Wall** bus make linear explorations of the Wall an easy prospect, and the National Park also runs an extensive series of guided walks in the vicinity.

A visit to **High Force** waterfall – the largest in England – can be made either by obtaining a ticket from the High Force Hotel, on the B6277 near Middleton-in-Teesdale, or walking up the Pennine Way from the (free) Wynch Bridge or Holwick Head Bridges, past Low Force.

Easy riders

Cycling and mountain biking

Kielder Forest and Water have become something of a Mecca for mountain bikers in recent years. Numerous trails are waymarked through the forest and handy guides are available from the cycle hire centres or the Tower Knowe Visitor centre. If you don't bring your own bike, you can hire one for a day or less from Kielder Bikes at the Cyclery, Castle Hill, Kielder or the Hawkhope Centre, Kielder Dam (tel: 01434 250392).

In Durham there are further woodland tracks ideal for mountain biking in the **Hamsterley Forest**. More ambitous cyclists might wish to try the **'C2C'** – an award-winning 140-mile (225km) national cycle route from the Irish Sea to the North Sea (Whitehaven and Workington in Cumbria to Sunderland), passing through the Durham Dales. For further details, tel: 01207 281259.

Horse-riding

A large number of bridleways suitable for horse-riders thread the Pennines and Cheviots, many of them very old routes used since medieval days by packhorses. The National Park Authority produces a list of local riding stables from where horses can be hired.

A new development has been the introduction of the **Border County Ride**, a 100-mile (160km) circular route through Kielder Forest and the Cheviots, waymarked by a white horseshoe on a blue background. Other popular waymarked routes include the **Cross Border Route**, from Newcastleton to Kielder, and the Blakehopeburn Route from Bryness through the Redesdale Forest.

Activities at Kielder

Watersports

Water sports of all kinds, including sailing and windsurfing, are also provided at Kielder, while there is good fishing for trout and salmon on the reservoirs and on the Rivers Tweed, Tees, Wear, North Tyne and Coquet. Rod licences are available on a daily basis from Northumbrian Water. Sea anglers find their sport along the Northumbrian coast, where the fishing is as fine as anywhere in Britain.

Sea angling at Seaham

Birdwatching

Northumberland is well served with opportunities for everyone from 'twitchers' to the less-obsessed. One of the favourite areas is the **Farne Islands**, where the last outcrops of the Whin Sill run out into the North Sea. In addition to a large resident population of grey seals, these rocky wave-splashed islands are alive with birds, including important colonies of puffins, eider ducks ('Cuddy's Ducks'), razorbills, cormorants, fulmars and kittiwakes. Ringed plovers and oystercatchers also nest here, along with guillemots and various terns, including the marathon-migrator, the arctic tern. The Farne Islands are in the care of the National Trust and can be reached by boat from Seahouses on the mainland coast.

Lapwing

There are also hides at the apparently unpromising **Kielder Water**, where a range of birds, from dippers in the streams to siskins and crossbills in the conifers, can be observed. Further south in County Durham, Castle Eden Dene near Peterlee is an English Nature Reserve famous for its summer migrants such as blackcaps and grasshopper warblers, and winter flocks of brambling, siskin, waxwing and the rare great grey shrike.

Getting There

By car

The A1 and A1(M) Great North Road provides fast and easy access from the south. Visitors coming from London can either use the A1 all the way, or the M1 as far as its junction with the M18 east of Sheffield, then join the A1(M). Coming from Scotland and the north, the A1 follows the coast from Edinburgh, or you can use the popular A68 cross-country route through the Southern Uplands and Border Country to Jedburgh and Carter Bar, before descending through Redesdale to Scotch Corner on the A1. From the west, the A66 provides a scenic cross-Pennine route from the M6, Cumbria and the Lake District. Further north, the A69 runs from Carlisle parallel with Hadrian's Wall to Newcastle and the A1(M).

Opposite: cyclists on the C2C route, County Durham

Fine tuning at Barnard Castle

By coach

National Express and other express coach services run daily from London and other major centres to Durham, Darlington, Newcastle and Carlisle. Services to Newcastle and Carlisle connect with the Northumbria bus service 685. Other local bus services connect Hexham with North Tynedale and the North Pennines, and there is a good network of local bus services in the area.

By train

Twenty-two high-speed InterCity trains run daily from London to Darlington and 14 to Durham and Newcastle. The journey takes between two and a half and three hours. For information and timetable enquiries, contact the InterCity East Coast office in Newcastle, tel: 0191 232 6262. The scenic Tyne Valley Regional Railways route links with InterCity services on both the east and west coast main lines, and with Durham and Sunderland (*see page 74*).

South Tynedale Railway

By air

Northumbria is easily accessible from Newcastle and Teeside Airports, which handle domestic flights to and from London Heathrow and Gatwick and other major regional airports, as well as most European destinations.

By sea

Regular ferry services link the region with Europe via the International Ferry Terminal at Royal Quays, North Shields, Tyneside. Ferries from Bergen and Stavanger are run by Color Lines (tel: 0191 296 1313); and from Gothenburg, Amsterdam and Hamburg by Scandinavian Seaways (tel: 0191 293 6262). North Sea Ferries services from Zeebrugge and Rotterdam use the port of Hull (tel: 01482 377177).

Getting Around

Buses

A good network of local bus services exists in Northumbria and the North Pennines, enabling the visitor to leave the car behind and enjoy the scenery without worrying about traffic and parking. Check with the local Tourist Information Centres for details, or ring the Northumberland National Park on 01434 605555; Northumberland County Council Public Transport Helpline on 01670 533128; the Public Transport Group, Durham County Council, on 0191 383 3337; the Cumbria County Council Public Transport Team on 01228 606000; or Tyne and Wear Passenger Transport's Travel line on 0191 232 5325.

To Blanchland by bus

'I came, I saw, I caught the bus...' The publicity slogan for the Hadrian's Wall bus adapts Julius Caesar's famous saying, and it certainly provides an excellent way to enjoy linear walks along the Wall. You can 'Hike with Hadrian' by using this convenient service, organised jointly by the Northumberland National Park, Tynedale Council and Cumbria County Council, which operates between April and October. Service 682 operates westwards from Carlisle to Vindolanda, while Service 890 travels east, starting from Hexham and overlapping with the 682, travelling to Greenhead. Both connect with rail and other bus services at Haltwhistle.

Coach tours are run by Busways Travel Services of Newcastle (tel: 0191 232 3918); Garfield Travel of Choppington (tel: 01670 815496); The Northern Nomad of Bracepeth, Durham (tel: 0191 3789809); and Safari Travel of Hetton-le-Hole (tel: 0191 5262003).

Trains

The scenic Tyne Valley Regional Railways route enables the visitor to explore the length of Hadrian's Wall and the beautiful Tyne Valley. Running between Whitehaven on the Cumbrian coast and Newcastle, Sunderland and Durham, the route passes through Carlisle and runs parallel with the Wall. There are stations at Corbridge, Hexham, Haydon Bridge, Bardon Mill and Haltwhistle, where the line links with the Hadrian's Wall bus service (*see above*). Enquiries, tel: 0345 484950.

Plotting a route in Hexham

Maps

The best maps to cover the area are the Ordnance Survey's 1:25,000 scale Outdoor Leisure series, of which four will be needed: No 16 (The Cheviot Hills); No 42 (Kielder Water); No 43 (Hadrian's Wall); and No 31 (North Pennines: Teesdale and Weardale). There is also the 1:25,000 OS Explorer No 1, which covers Kielder Water, and the OS Historical Map and Guide, which covers Hadrian's Wall.

Facts for the Visitor

Tourist and visitor information

The area is well served with visitor and tourist information centres, most of which operate the 'BABA' (Book a Bed Ahead) system for the visitors' convenience. The major tourist information and National Park visitor centres are as follows (note that those marked by * operate during the summer season only):

Alnwick, The Shambles, tel: 01665 510665; **Barnard Castle,** Flatts Road, tel: 01833 690909; **Beamish,** Open Air Museum, tel: 0191 370 2533; **Bellingham,** Main Street, tel: 01434 220616; **Berwick,** Castlegate Car Park, tel: 01289 330733; **Bishop Auckland,** The Town Hall, Market Place, tel: 01388 604922; ***Corbridge,** Hill Street, tel: 01434 632815; ***Craster,** Car Park, tel: 01665 57007; **Durham,** Market Place, tel: 0191 384 3720; **Haltwhistle,** Westgate, tel: 01434 322002; **Hexham,** Hallgate, tel: 01434 605225; **Jarrow,** The Museum, tel: 0191 4892106; **Morpeth,** Bridge Street, tel: 01670 511323; ***Once Brewed,** Bardon Mill, tel: 01434 344396; **Peterlee,** Upper Chare, tel: 0191 586 4450; **Prudhoe,** Waterworld, Front Street, tel: 01661 833144; ***Rothbury,** Church Street, tel: 01669 620887; ***Seahouses,** Car Park, tel: 01665 720884; **South Shields,** Museum and Art Gallery, tel: 0191 4546612; **Stanhope,** Durham Dales Centre, tel: 01388 527650; **Whitley Bay,** Park Road, tel: 0191 2008535; ***Wooler,** High Street, tel: 01668 28160.

The **Northumberland National Park** headquarters is at Eastburn, South Park, Hexham, tel: 01434 605555, and the **National Trust's** Northumbria headquarters is at Scot's Gap, Morpeth, tel: 01670 774691. The **Northumbria Tourist Board's** headquarters is at Aykley Heads, Durham DH1 SUX, tel: 0191 375 3000.

Emergencies

For any emergency requiring police, fire or ambulance services, dial 999 from any telephone and ask for the service you require. There are casualty departments at the major hospitals in Newcastle, Sunderland, Durham and Darlington.

Market days

Alnwick: Saturday; **Amble**: Sunday; **Barnard Castle**: Wednesday; **Berwick**: Wednesday and Saturday; **Bishop Auckland**: Thursday and Saturday; **Chester-le-Street**: Tuesday and Friday; **Darlington**: Monday and Saturday; **Durham**: Thursday to Saturday; **Haltwhistle**: Thursday; **Hexham**: Tuesday; **Middleton-in-Teesdale**: Tuesday; **Morpeth**: Monday and Wednesday; **Newcastle-upon-Tyne**: Tuesday, Thursday and Saturday.

A good place to start in Durham

Market stall in Middleton

Down the mine at Beamish

Northumbria for children

The Northumberland National Park has a well-developed education and interpretation service which produces an exciting annual programme of **events, activities and guided walks**, many of which are aimed at younger visitors. A typical example is the 'Roman Clue Trail' along Hadrian's Wall from Walltown. Details are given in the Park's *What's On* booklet.

Among the commercial attractions which have a special appeal for children, the finest is undoubtedly the **North of England Open Air Museum** at Beamish (for details and opening times, *see Route 7, page 51*).

Children will also enjoy the exciting and imaginative reconstructions of what life was really like on Hadrian's Wall by a visit to the **Roman Army Museum** (*see Route 5, page 39*), **Vindolanda** (*see page 40*) and the **Birdoswald Roman Fort** at Gisland, near Brampton (April 1 to October 31, 10am to 5.30pm).

Washing ore at Killhope

The region's lead mining past is very well interpreted for young and old at the **Killhope Lead Mining Centre** in Weardale (*see Route 8, page 59*) and at the **Nenthead Mines** near Alston (*see Route 8, page 58*). In Alston the **South Tynedale Railway** runs regular steam and diesel-hauled passenger trips beside the river (*see Route 8, page 58*), and children will also enjoy a trip on the world's oldest existing steam railway to the oldest surviving railway bridge at Causey Arch, on the 3-mile (5km) **Tanfield Railway** near Stanley (daily 10am–5pm).

Countryside interests are well served by the newly-opened **Otter Trust's North Pennines Reserve** near Bowes (28 March to 31 October, 10.30am–6pm), and the **Butterfly Farm** at Tow Law Nursery (Easter to 30 September, 10am–5pm).

Accommodation

Northumbria has a wealth of fine country house hotels, and most villages have bed-and-breakfast accommodation. It is always advisable to book ahead, especially in the summer season, and this is easily done by using one of the tourist information centres listed on page 75. Comprehensive accommodation guides covering the region are produced annually by the Northumbria Tourist Board, tel: 0191 375 3000; Durham County Council, tel: 0191 383 3354; Tynedale Council, tel: 01434 605225; and the North Pennines Tourism Partnership, tel: 01434 382069.

Youth Hostels are situated at Alston, Baldersdale, Barnard Castle, Dufton, Edmundbyers, Greenhead, Langdon Beck, Middleton-in-Teesdale, Newcastle-upon-Tyne, Once Brewed, Bardon Mill, and Wooler.

Orchard Guest House in Rothbury

The following is a selective list of some of the hotels and guesthouses in the region, most of which also offer extra value Northumbria Breaks including two nights dinner and bed and breakfast. Costs per night per room are: £££ = over £80; ££ = over £50, and £ = up to £50.

Alnmouth
Marine House Hotel, Marine Road, Alnmouth, tel: 01665 830349. Former guests at this ivy-clad 200-year-old listed building facing the golf links and the sea include Charles Dickens. £. **Saddle Hotel**, Northumberland Street, Alnmouth, tel: 01665 830476. This family-run hotel is also one of Alnmouth's premier eating places. £.

Alnwick
Masons Arms, Stamford, near Rennington, Alnwick, tel: 01665 577275. A former coaching inn on the B1340 between Alnwick and Seahouses, providing excellent accommodation in converted stables. £. **White Swan Hotel**, Bondgate Within, Alnwick, tel: 01665 602109. Offers modern facilities in traditional Georgian elegance. £. **Dunstanburgh Castle Hotel**, Embleton, Alnwick, tel: 01665 576111. In the centre of the little village of Embleton and 10 minutes walk from the golden Embleton Sands. £.

The White Swan in Alnwick

Barnard Castle
Rose and Crown Hotel, Romaldkirk, Barnard Castle, tel: 01833 650213. An 18th-century coaching inn in the centre of one of Teesdale's prettiest villages, with good English cooking. ££. **Jersey Farm Hotel**, Darlington Road, Barnard Castle, tel: 01833 638223. A four crowns, highly commended hotel just over a mile east of the town centre. ££. **Montalbo Hotel**, Montalbo Road, Barnard Castle, tel: 01833 637342. Another commended hotel, this time in the town centre and convenient for the castle. £.

Victoria Hotel, Bamburgh

Bamburgh

Victoria Hotel, Front Street, Bamburgh, tel: 01668 214431. Fine old hotel overlooking the village green with individually designed rooms and play den for children. ££. **Sunningdale Hotel**, Lucker Road, Bamburgh, tel: 01668 214334. This family-run hotel offers special dinner, bed and breakfast rates throughout July and August. £.

Bellingham

Riverdale Hall Hotel, Bellingham, tel: 01434 220254. A country house hotel with extensive grounds, indoor swimming pool, sauna and trout and salmon fishing in the North Tyne. £££. **Cheviot Hotel**, Bellingham, tel: 01434 220696. All rooms are en suite in this family-run hotel. £.

Berwick-upon-Tweed

Marshall Meadows Country House Hotel, Berwick, tel: 01289 331133. The most northerly hotel in England, this elegant Georgian mansion is set in 15 acres of grounds and is 10 minutes from the centre of Berwick. £.

Centre of Britian Hotel, Haltwhistle

Blanchland

Lord Crewe Arms Hotel, Blanchland, tel: 01434 675251. One of the most characterful hotels in Northumbria. Formerly the lodgings of the Abbot of Blanchland Abbey, guests are greeted with blazing log fires, stone-flagged floors and a large choice of beers in the Crypt Bar. ££.

Durham

Royal County Hotel, Old Elvet, Durham, tel: 0191 386 6821. A four-star hotel in the centre of Durham with an award-winning restaurant. ££. **Three Tuns Hotel**, New Elvet, Durham, tel: 0191 386 4326. Another central hotel in an ancient inn. ££.

Falstone

The Pheasant Inn, Stannerburn, Falstone, tel: 01434 240382. Convenient for Kielder Water and the Borders, this 300-year-old country inn has beamed ceilings and stone walls in its eight en-suite bedrooms. £.

Haltwhistle

Centre of Britain Hotel, Haltwhistle, tel: 01434 320391. A new hotel created from an ancient 15th-century pele tower, excise house and coaching station. £.

Hexham

Slaley Hall, Slaley, Hexham, tel: 01434 673350. Situated in a 1,000-acre (400 hectare) estate, complete with 18-hole championship golf course, Slaley Hall is an Edwardian mansion which offers luxury accommodation and food.

£££. **The George Swallow Hotel**, Chollerford, Hexham, tel: 01434 681611. A fine restaurant and lovely setting by the bridge over the North Tyne give this large, 46-bed hotel a special atmosphere. ££. **Langley Castle Hotel**, Langley-on-Tyne, Hexham, tel: 01434 688888. Housed in a 14th-century fortified manor house, with 16 well-appointed bedrooms and fine restaurant. ££. **Beaumont Hotel**, Beaumont Street, Hexham, tel: 01434 602331. A three-star AA family-run hotel overlooking the abbey. ££.

Middleton-in-Teesdale
Teesdale Hotel, Middleton-in-Teesdale, tel: 01833 640264/640537. Housed in a Grade II listed 17th-century coaching inn in the heart of Teesdale, this mullion-windowed hotel welcomes pets and children. ££.

Teesdale Hotel, Middleton

Otterburn
Percy Arms Hotel, Otterburn, tel: 01830 520261. On the banks of the River Rede, the kitchen boasts home produced smoked foods and 'calorie laden' sweets. £.

Rothbury
Whitton Farmhouse Hotel, Rothbury, tel: 01669 620811. A country house hotel overlooking the valley of the Coquet which offers riding from its own stables. £. **Silverton Lodge**, Silverton Lane, Rothbury, tel: 01669 620144. Delightful hotel housed in a former village schoolhouse on the edge of Rothbury. £. **Orchard Guest House**, High Street, Rothbury, tel: 01669 620684. Highly commended and centrally situated, an excellent centre for touring. £.

79

Seahouses
The Olde Ship Hotel, Main Street, Seahouses, tel: 01665 720200. The bars and lounges house a unique collection of maritime memorabilia in this 12 bedroomed, traditonal hotel overlooking the harbour. £. **St Aiden Hotel**, Sea Front, Seahouses, tel: 01665 720355. Superb sea views from the Farne Islands to Bamburgh Castle make this one of the best situated hotels on the heritage coast. £.

Warkworth
Warkworth House Hotel, Bridge Street, Warkworth, tel: 01665 711276. Some of the bedrooms in this splendid Georgian-fronted hotel boast their own ghosts, but the atmosphere is always friendly. £.

Wooler
Tankerville Arms, Cottage Road, Wooler, tel: 01668 281581. An ivy-clad, 17th-century former coaching inn, just off the A697 near the centre of this market town, convenient for the Cheviots and Borders. £.

Warkworth House Hotel